Praise for Twitter *Power 3.0*

"This book outlines, describes and creates a path to discover how to build your business and brand using the most publicly shared platform in social media today. As Twitter evolves so has this incredible book series into the third and most powerful evolution. Joel and Mark swung for the fences and knocked it out of the park on this one."

—Bryan Kramer, TED presenter, author of *Human to Human* and CEO at PureMatter, @bryankramer

"Twitter is the FIRE in our social media strategy, and Joel Comm's *Twitter Power* creates an inferno! It is *the* go-to resource for Twitter, and I would never *ignite* without it!"

—John Lee Dumas of EntrepreneurOnFire, @johnleedumas

"If you want to understand how Twitter can help you expand your contacts and grow your sales, purchase and devour this book."

—Michael Stelzner, founder of Social Media Examiner, @Mike_Stelzner

"What I learned from @JoelComm: Twitter = Power! Twitter Power 3.0 is the triple threat!"

—Lori Ruff, ~~Forbes top so~~ uencer, @LoriRuff

D0973042

"If, like Joel Comm, you ~~...~~ rsonal life, in the company of those ~~...~~ ctly how to leverage your *Twitter Po* ~~...~~ ed bestseller. Comm is living proof th ~~... more~~ meaningful, fun and profitable life with others by socially participating in Twitter with a mutuality mindset that proves you believe in creating opportunities with and for others. Like a legion of others, I have directly benefitted from his friendship, and I love his actionable insights in this book."

—Kare Anderson, TED presenter, author of *Mutuality Matters*, and *Forbes* and *Huffington Post* columnist, @kareanderson

This is a gift from the:

Danville Library Foundation

DANVILLE LIBRARY FOUNDATION

"Twitter is undoubtedly the most powerful tool a business and brand can use to create meaningful connections with its customers. It's not about pushing out a message, but providing value, helping, and most importantly, listening to your customers on a direct, personal level, which ultimately builds incredible brand loyalty. No one knows this better than Joel Comm, who literally wrote (and rewrote) *the book* on Twitter. More than just about *how* and *why*, Joel understands and is able to teach others how to leverage the power of Twitter using advanced tactics and strategies that are applicable to individuals, small businesses, and big brands alike. Joel shows his knowledge and years of experience in an easy-to-understand, and immediately actionable format. *Twitter Power 3.0* is required reading, and a must-have in any business's online toolbox."

—Lou Mongello, Disney expert, author, podcast host, speaker, and entrepreneur, @LouMongello

"Twitter is one of the major platforms I leveraged that got me my start for building an online business and Joel was one of the guys I followed to see how it was done. This is a powerful resource you'll wanna have!"

—Lewis Howes, The School of Greatness Podcast, @LewisHowes

"A huge Twitter fan, I have seen the power of this truly social network in building connections and igniting brand love. Whether it is your personal brand or your company brand, Twitter is a phenomenal tool for establishing human and authentic touchpoints and building brand advocacy. This book is a must-read!"

—Ekaterina Walter, global evangelist at Sprinklr, author of the *Wall Street Journal* bestseller *Think Like Zuck*, and co-author of *The Power of Visual Storytelling*, @ekaterina

"Social Media is great, but socializing is even better! Nobody does it more successfully than Joel. What he writes, you cannot miss reading . . . it's that simple."

—Ted Rubin, social marketing strategist, keynote speaker, brand evangelist, and acting CMO at Brand Innovators, @TedRubin

"Twitter and social media are like having an ATM in your pocket. The power of building relationships, and engaging and networking with people at all hours of the day is enormous. And, does lead to huge dollars over time. We do an estimated $750,000 per year through social media and that's without any paid advertising. Some of the key strategies I have learned come from Joel and his brilliance about Twitter. If you are not engaged in social media, you are missing out on significant dollars for your business!"

—Colin Sprake, CEO and business Sherpa, @colinsprake

"Joel has done it again! In this book he once again reveals the latest tips and wisdom needed to successfully navigate the social media waters. Soak it in and apply his expertise as it is priceless."

—Tony Rubleski, bestselling author,
MindCaptureGroup.com, @mindcapture

"Joel Comm is a sparkling ray of brilliance in the social media universe and *Twitter Power 3.0* is your personal ticket to reach the stars. Grab this book now, so you don't miss the ride to the top!"

—Ken McArthur, bestselling author of *Impact: How to Get Noticed,
Motivate Millions and Make a Difference in a Noisy World*, @kenmcarthur

"Really since the beginning of the "social" revolution, Joel Comm has been one of our thought leaders—and *Twitter Power* one of our business manifestos. I'm excited about the new release relevant to all the shifts and changes social has undergone!"

—Viveka von Rosen, @LinkedInExpert

"Joel Comm did it again. This global pioneer on Twitter engagement writes yet another blockbuster that dives deep into the human psyche on how to masterfully engage in social media. Whether you're brand new to Twitter or have already attracted a large following, Joel's authentic and riveting advice will increase your Twitter influence and capture your heart, as well."

—Shawne Duperon, six-time Emmy winner,
Project: Forgive founder, @ shawnetv

"Twitter Power is pure marketing gold! If you are looking to finally get REAL results from Twitter-ville, this is a must read! Apply Joel's step-by-step how-tos and watch your business soar."

—Kim Garst, Forbes Top 50 Influencer, @kimgarst

"Social media is the most important topic of the decade. Twitter is the most cost-effective at driving new potential buyers to your website. And Joel Comm is one of most effective and consistently cutting-edge authorities on Internet marketing in the world. *Twitter Power* is a unique book guaranteed to have a dramatic effect on your business's bottom line."

—Brian Carter, digital marketing consultant, keynote speaker, @briancarter

"I see tremendous value in the power of Twitter as an additional platform to connect, engage, and build authentic relationships. Joel Comm is brilliant at teaching how Twitter can be integrated into existing marking strategies to build a loyal following."

—Sue B. Zimmerman, captain of online branding, @suebzimmerman

twitter power 3.0

How to Dominate Your Market
ONE TWEET AT A TIME

JOEL COMM & DAVE TAYLOR

WITHDRAWN

WILEY

Cover design: Matt Clark @TweetPages (another creative smile by ImageDesigns)

Copyright © 2015 by Infomedia, Inc. and Dave Taylor. All rights reserved.

Published by John Wiley & Sons, Inc., Hoboken, New Jersey.
Published simultaneously in Canada.

No part of this publication may be reproduced, stored in a retrieval system, or transmitted in any form or by any means, electronic, mechanical, photocopying, recording, scanning, or otherwise, except as permitted under Section 107 or 108 of the 1976 United States Copyright Act, without either the prior written permission of the Publisher, or authorization through payment of the appropriate per-copy fee to the Copyright Clearance Center, 222 Rosewood Drive, Danvers, MA 01923, (978) 750-8400, fax (978) 646-8600, or on the Web at www .copyright.com. Requests to the Publisher for permission should be addressed to the Permissions Department, John Wiley & Sons, Inc., 111 River Street, Hoboken, NJ 07030, (201) 748-6011, fax (201) 748-6008, or online at www.wiley.com/go/permissions.

Limit of Liability/Disclaimer of Warranty: While the publisher and author have used their best efforts in preparing this book, they make no representations or warranties with the respect to the accuracy or completeness of the contents of this book and specifically disclaim any implied warranties of merchantability or fitness for a particular purpose. No warranty may be created or extended by sales representatives or written sales materials. The advice and strategies contained herein may not be suitable for your situation. You should consult with a professional where appropriate. Neither the publisher nor the author shall be liable for damages arising herefrom.

For general information about our other products and services, please contact our Customer Care Department within the United States at (800) 762-2974, outside the United States at (317) 572-3993 or fax (317) 572-4002.

Wiley publishes in a variety of print and electronic formats and by print-on-demand. Some material included with standard print versions of this book may not be included in e-books or in print-on-demand. If this book refers to media such as a CD or DVD that is not included in the version you purchased, you may download this material at http://booksupport.wiley.com. For more information about Wiley products, visit www.wiley.com.

Library of Congress Cataloging-in-Publication Data:

Comm, Joel.
   Twitter power 3.0: how to dominate your market one tweet at a time/Joel Comm, Dave Taylor. — Third edition.
      pages cm
Revision of the author's Twitter power 2.0.
Includes index.
   ISBN 978-1-119-02181-0 (paperback: alk. paper); ISBN 978-1-119-05007-0 (ebk); ISBN 978-1-119-05011-7 (ebk)
   1. Twitter. 2. Internet marketing. 3. Business communication. 4. Online social networks. I. Taylor, Dave, 1962- II. Comm, Joel. Twitter power. III. Title.
   HF5415.1265.C646 2015
   658.8'72—dc23

2014044787

Printed in the United States of America.

10 9 8 7 6 5 4 3 2 1

Contents

Foreword

I started on Twitter in August 2007 after exhortations from some friends. At first I didn't get it: "Why do I care if LonelyBoy15's cat rolled over?" The light went on when I started searching for my name, people I knew, and topics that interested me.

Seven years later, I've connected with people from all over the world. I have 1.4 million followers and have tweeted 132,000 times. Sometimes I tweet when my dog rolls over, too. Twitter has become a fantastic tool for me.

You don't need to spend seven years and 132,000 tweets to learn how to use Twitter because Joel Comm and Dave Taylor have written *Twitter Power 3.0: How to Dominate Your Market One Tweet at a Time*. Lucky you! I wish it had been that easy for me.

This book will give you a big head start toward mastering Twitter from two people who already have. So buy this book, read it, and then go forth and tweet up a storm!

—Guy Kawasaki, chief evangelist for Canva

INTRODUCTION

It seems like just yesterday that my publisher asked me to write the first edition of *Twitter Power*. With just more than 5,000 followers to my name in 2008, I was an early adopter of the now-ubiquitous social media site known for 140-character posts.

It thrills me that the first and second editions of *Twitter Power* have become the top-selling books in the world on the subject of using Twitter! I knew that Twitter was onto something, but I never imagined that it would become such a significant part of our culture.

The hashtag is now a part of our discourse and has influenced many other social media sites to include hashtag support on their service.

The Twittersphere's ability to discover and broadcast breaking news faster than any of the major networks makes every member a potential man or woman on the street.

The connection we feel with musicians, celebrities, politicians, athletes, and authors has never been greater because Twitter has allowed us to interact with some of the people whom everyone knows.

And businesses are discovering that Twitter is an incredibly powerful branding tool useful for engaging with prospects and customers, as well as providing top-quality customer support.

With more than 250 million monthly active Twitter members and a member base exceeding 1 billion accounts, the Twitter hashtag and well-known *@username* appear on television shows, in film promotions, on billboards, in magazines, and in a variety of other promotional materials.

Twitter is everywhere, and it is here to stay.

And although the 140-character limit hasn't changed, much has evolved since the release of *Twitter Power 2.0* in 2010.

Lists for organizing those you follow, the ability to embed photos and images in your tweets, an official Twitter advertising system designed to help businesses engage and drive followers to take specific action, and a better understanding of how Twitter members like to engage are just some of the new things covered in this book.

One of the other changes to this completely updated and revised third edition is the addition of a coauthor, Dave Taylor (of AskDaveTaylor.com). A prolific author of many business and technical books, Dave has been a good friend of mine for many years. Because of his involvement in the social space, I thought it would be fun for us to coauthor this book. To avoid confusing you, the reader, as to who is speaking, we refer to ourselves in the third person throughout the book.

So, whether you are a seasoned Twitter user, someone who has dabbled in tweeting from time to time, or a complete newbie to Twitter, you are in for a treat. Dave and I believe this is the best edition of *Twitter Power* yet, and we're excited for you to jump in and discover how to make your Twitter experience as great as possible!

If you use Twitter to connect with friends or family, or if you manage a Twitter account for your own small business or as part of a large corporate team, the pages that follow are dedicated to helping you leverage the power of Twitter like never before.

Who knew 140 characters could be so powerful?

—Joel Comm

An Introduction to the Social Media Landscape

Once upon a time, anyone could be a media publisher. All you needed was several million dollars, a team of editors and writers, a printing press capable of shooting out a dozen copies a second, and a distribution network that would put your publication in stores across the country.

Unless, of course, you wanted to go into radio or television. In that case, things were just a little harder.

The result was that information came down from on high. We didn't talk among ourselves, and we weren't part of the conversation; we were talked *to* by writers, editors, and producers who controlled the conversation. If we liked what we were reading, we kept tuning in, and the publishing company made money.

If we didn't like it, we stopped buying the magazine, or we switched channels. Advertisers turned away, and all the millions of dollars the publication took to create disappeared.

Today, it's all very different. It now costs as little as nothing more than time to create great content and make it available for other people to enjoy. That low cost means that it doesn't matter if millions or even thousands do not read it if your target market is smaller or nascent. The rise of social media means you can profitably focus on even tiny markets—such as stamp collectors in Mozambique—and still find enough people to form an online community and profit through advertising and product sales.

The buzzword for this rise of small and micro communities, as *Wired* editor Chris Anderson coined it, is *the long tail*, and it's absolutely been rocket fuel for our Internet race to the moon.

But the lowered barrier to entry for publishing online has had another positive effect: We aren't being talked to by professional writers and publishers anymore; we're talking to each other.

Average folk like you and me—the kind of people who didn't study writing at college, who never spent years as cub reporters covering local court cases or high school sports, and who were never even very good at Scrabble or Words with Friends—are now writing about the topics they love and sharing their views and opinions online.

And they're hearing from their readers, too. The conversation is flowing in both directions.

Anyone can now launch a website or blog, write articles, share their thoughts and views on Facebook or other social media, or even create videos and upload them to YouTube. And anyone can comment on that content, affecting both its nature and the direction of the publication.

That's social media; it's a publishing revolution, and we're smack-dab in the middle of it!

What Exactly Is Social Media?

Social media can be all sorts of different things, and it can be produced in all sorts of different ways. Perhaps the best definition of social media, though, is content that has been created cooperatively with its audience.

Facebook, for example, is not a publishing company. It doesn't create any of its own content. It doesn't write articles or posts, and it doesn't upload films or images for people to view and enjoy.

It allows its users to do all of that for their own amusement, edification, and profit. Facebook is a platform, a set of tools that enable this activity.

It's as though the National Broadcasting Company (NBC) or Showtime were to fire all its actors, producers, news anchors, and scriptwriters; throw open its doors; and tell the world that all are welcome to come in, shoot their own programs, and broadcast them on the channel. Or as though *People* magazine were to open its pages up to anyone who wanted to publish a photograph or write some celebrity gossip. That would be sweet, wouldn't it?

Of course, if that were to happen, you'd still have to tell people what channel you were on and when they could see your program. You'd still have to produce content that other people might actually enjoy and, inevitably, the people who took the most professional approach, put time and effort into what they were doing, and connected with their audiences would be the most successful.

But even that wouldn't allow viewers to take part in the program, to participate in the creation of something bigger than a video segment or article in the next issue of the magazine. That participation is the cornerstone of social media.

Create a group on a site such as Facebook, and you won't need to supply all of the text and all of the images to keep it lively and interesting. You'll be expecting other group members to add their stories and photographs, to engage in discussions, and to share their own experiences.

Even bloggers, when they write a post, hope that their readers will join the discussion by leaving comments at the bottom of the post, taking the conversation in new directions and adding new information and perspectives.

This is the *social* part of social media, and it means that publishing is now about participation.

Let's say that again because it's so darn important to *Twitter Power* and to success on social media in any venue: *publishing is now about participation.*

Someone who uses social media successfully doesn't just create content; he or she also creates conversations, and those conversations create communities.

That's the real beauty of social media, and although creating a separate community may or may not be a primary goal— depending on the site—the result of social media can always be solid connections among participants.

When those connections form around businesses, the results can be the sort of brand loyalty and commitment that sales professionals have been dreaming about since the first days of direct marketing.

We'll admit it; our definition of social media is rather vague. At its broadest, it describes a form of publishing in which people swap rather than publish stories and the exchange of content happens within a community, rather like a chat in a restaurant.

At its narrowest, it describes a tool set that lets publishers and marketers put their messages in front of thousands of people and encourage them to build strong connections and firm loyalty.

However it's defined, social media has proved incredibly popular!

As of September 2014, Facebook claims to have 864 million active daily members—that's *active* members, not just people who created a profile and never used it—and 703 million active daily mobile users. Expand the data to monthly active users, and there are more than 1.3 billion people busily posting and discussing things in the Facebook community. That's billion with a *b*.

Twitter, which launched almost a decade ago—a lifetime in Internet terms—has similarly impressive statistics, and its growth has been phenomenal. As of this writing in late 2014, Twitter has 271 million active users, 78 percent of whom are on mobile devices. Together, we send more than 500 million tweets per day, and the system supports more than 35 languages.

Helped by the appearance on the site of celebrities, such as Katy Perry, Taylor Swift, Rihanna, Ellen DeGeneres, Britney Spears, Ashton Kutcher, and Oprah Winfrey (who posted her first tweet live on her TV show, assisted by Twitter cofounder Evan Williams), Twitter's growth chart has changed from a gentle climb into a hockey stick, a phenomenal accomplishment.

There is another fact about Twitter that's particularly interesting, though: It's massively underused.

The average Twitterer has 126 followers and has sent out fewer than 300 tweets across the life of his or her account. Not only that, but 30 to 40 percent of Twitter accounts are also dormant, never having posted a single tweet.

To put a few numbers here, Joel currently has 81,119 followers and follows 1,372 people, and Dave has 12,574 followers and follows 932 people. And to put things in perspective, when Joel was asked to write the first edition of *Twitter Power* back in 2009, he had only 5,000 followers, and not a single person had yet come close to having 1 million followers.

Twitter's growth has turned it into a massive marketing opportunity.

All of these figures just scratch the surface of the popularity of social media, though. YouTube attracts more than 1 billion unique visitors each month. Visitors watch more than 6 billion hours of video content each month. Oh, and 100 hours of video are uploaded to YouTube every minute. Every minute!

Throw in the countless millions of blogs and social networks, such as Pinterest, Instagram, Google Plus, and Reddit, and it becomes pretty clear that social media is a massive phenomenon that's changed the way all of us create and use content—and the way that businesses use that content and their distribution channels, too.

Social Media Really Is a Big Deal

So we can see that social media sites and users can be big. Really, really big. But so what? There are lots of people in the telephone book, and that's very big, too. Being big doesn't make it a particularly useful marketing tool.

Social media sites don't just list people, though, and they don't just list any old people.

Each site lists a very special group of people.

At first glance, that might seem a little strange. Whether you're browsing through Facebook, Pinterest, Flickr, or Twitter, you're going to see small pictures of people, short messages among them, and profiles in which those people share things about themselves, such as where they work, where they're from, and what they do in their spare time.

Look a little closer, though, and you'll start to notice differences because although the sites may seem similar, in fact, each site has its own unique feel and its own unique demographic.

Because Facebook started at Harvard University, for example (it had signed up half the undergraduate population within a month of going live), and because it was initially restricted to university students, it continues to have a higher percentage of well-educated members than of the general population.

Clearly, that suggests many of Facebook's users are also college students—a fantastic market for companies hoping to acquire buyers and fans, then turn them into invaluable lifetime customers and evangelists.

By comparison, tracking Twitter's demographics isn't easy. Although some people have had fun following the frequency with which certain wealth-related terms (such as *well-to-do neighborhoods*) turn up, there's no easy way to conduct a demographic survey of the site's users. Hitwise, an Internet monitoring service, did, however, manage to produce some very interesting, and some very impressive, results.

Figure 1.1 shows some Twitter stats from the company.

Pew Internet reports that as of January 2014, 18 percent of online adults use Twitter, broken down into 17 percent of online

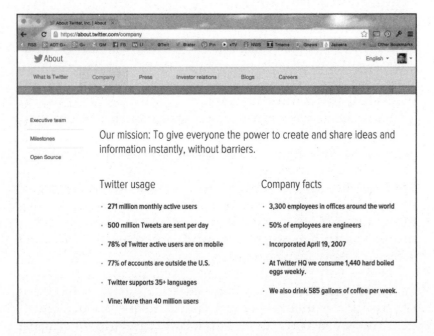

Figure 1.1   Now you know how much coffee they consume at Twitter's headquarters!

adult males and 18 percent of online women, with 16 percent of white, 29 percent of African American, and 16 percent of Hispanic ethnicities represented. Twitter also biases younger: 31 percent of users are 18- to 29-year-olds, 19 percent are 30 to 49, and less than 10 percent are older than 50.

Most fascinating of all, though, 18 percent of Twitter users have completed some college, and another 18 percent have an undergrad or graduate degree. When you consider earnings, the greatest percentage of online users who are on Twitter are those who earn $75,000 or more. That's a lot of dough!

Although a number of twentysomethings might have joined Twitter out of curiosity, it is clear that the site isn't just used by young people as an alternative to text messaging and Facebook chats. Twitter has a large following among older, professional audiences, and a full quarter of Twitter's users are high earners, a valuable piece of information that makes the service a must for any serious marketer.

We can see that social media sites aren't just attracting kids looking for places to chat with their friends and find out where to load up on free music downloads. They're also attracting smart, educated people with money to burn.

They're attracting experts, too.

You can see this most clearly on specialist sites, such as Flickr, a photo-sharing service. Although Flickr too isn't very forthcoming about its demographic details, spend any time at all on the site, and you can't help but notice the number of professional photographers who use it.

Part of the site's appeal isn't just the pictures; enthusiasts also can pick up advice from experts who are working in their field and are ready to share the benefits of their experience.

Whatever site we look at, there's no question at this point in the evolution of the Internet that social media sites attract huge numbers of people. We can see too that many of those people are highly educated, are well paid, and are experts in their fields.

You should be realizing that social media offers a gigantic opportunity for business owners to promote their products to exactly the sort of market they want to reach, whether it's predominantly male, female, rich, poor, geographically based, or of a specific ethnic group.

The Different Types of Social Media Sites—Content to Suit Every Market

One of the reasons that social media has proved to be so popular is that it's available in all sorts of different forms. Although the networking sites with their tens of millions of members might be the most familiar, there are actually all sorts of different ways of creating and sharing social media content.

BLOGS

Yes, blogs are a form of social media, too. They're written by people on every topic you can imagine. (See Figure 1.2.) And only a tiny fraction of them are produced by professionals, even though all have the potential to generate revenue. Figure 1.2 is Joel's blog.

Figure 1.2 Joel's blog's home page at JoelComm.com. He writes it; you read it and comment on it. And yes, Comm is his real last name!

Meanwhile, Dave has three blogs. Really! Check out GoFatherhood.com to learn about his life as a dad, visit DaveOnFilm.com to read his film reviews, and then hang out at AskDaveTaylor.com to read his daily tech questions and answers and product reviews!

What really makes blogging part of social media is that it has incredibly minimal costs associated with getting started and running your site. Sure, if you want to have your own domain name and place the blog on your own server, you might have to pay a small fee—and when we say *small*, we mean less than $10 per month. There are strategies you can use to bring in readers that will cost money, too.

But you don't actually *need* to do any of that.

To become a blogger, you don't need to do any more than sign up at Blogger.com, WordPress.com, or any of the other free blogging services and start writing.

Within minutes, you'll be creating content, and you'll form a part of the social media world.

Blogs, though, do take some effort. They have to be updated regularly, and although you can put anything on a blog, from favorite quotes to short stories to feature-length videos, you'll have to work to keep your readers entertained, informed, and engaged. Blogging is fun and can be very profitable, too, but it's not a sweat-free business.

Most important, although you can accept guest posts and hire writers, and although your comments will be a crucial element of your site's attraction, it will still be *you* guiding the content and setting the subjects.

Blogs *are* a form of social media, but blogging is a society with a clear ruler, someone who has to head to the mines every morning and work for those gems. They don't just fall into your lap!

MEMBERSHIP SITES

That top-down feel that can be present in some social media channels is also present in membership sites. There are far fewer of these on the Web than there are blogs, but there's still no

Figure 1.3   All dating sites are membership sites.

shortage of them; like any social media site, they rely on the members to produce the content and discussion that serves as the site's primary attraction.

A great example of a membership site is Match.com. In fact, all dating sites are a narrowly targeted form of social media, with people identifying their own attributes as they sign up, as shown in Figure 1.3. The content that people are paying to use are the profiles and pictures that the site's members have created and uploaded.

Match.com might have an online magazine, but no one is paying $20 to $25 per month to read the magazine. Users are paying that price month after month to read the descriptions and look at the photos that other people have posted, and to contact those people.

It's not the site that's the attraction of social media sites; it's the society.

Photo Sites

Ever since cameras went digital, there's been a need for a low-cost—and even free—way to share those images with anyone who wants to see them online. In addition to the millions of photos posted every day on Facebook, sites and services are dedicated just to photos and images, notably including Pinterest and Instagram.

What makes these sites, and photo gallery sites such as Flickr, so cool is that they're designed specifically around displaying and sharing photographs, so the presentation is bigger, bolder, and more visually engaging, all of which is good!

Let's focus on Flickr for just a moment, because it's the granddaddy of photo-sharing sites. As a social media site, it of course depends entirely on the photos that users upload to bring in other users. (See Figure 1.4.)

That broad-based content sourcing already makes sites such as Flickr—one of the most popular photo-sharing sites—part of the social media phenomenon, but Flickr also has the networking power of those sites.

Like Facebook, it's possible to create large lists of friends and join groups where you can submit images, enter competitions,

Figure 1.4   Flickr is the big daddy of photo-sharing websites.

and participate in discussions about the best way to light a child's portrait or which lens to use in which conditions.

Flickr also allows its members to mark images as favorites and to place comments beneath them. Both of those activities can be valuable ways of adding new friends. Pro members, who pay a subscription fee of $44.95 for two years, can even see stats that indicate how many views, faves, and comments each image has produced and even where their visitors came from.

All of that networking is vital to success on the site, and that success can have some spectacular results. Even way back in 2006, Rebekka Guðleifsdóttir, an Icelandic art student whose images and networking had brought her a huge following on Flickr, was spotted by an advertising executive on the site who hired her to shoot a series of billboard shots for the Toyota Prius. Many of the images used in various versions of Microsoft Windows were bought from photographers commissioned after they were discovered on the site.

Every day, images are licensed and prints are sold on Flickr, and it's all based on the content created by the site's users and promoted through careful networking.

That's classic social media.

MICROBLOGS

And finally, we come to microblogging. This is a whole new thing in social media, though teens have been embracing this low-attention-span-friendly social networking for years. In fact, in some ways it's the exact opposite of everything we've seen so far.

Social media sites tend to want their members to contribute as much content as possible. They may restrict that content to just photographs or video (e.g., Flickr and Pinterest), restrict it to participating in the site only through a mobile device (e.g., Instagram), or restrict membership to a select few (in the case of dating sites, to dedicated singles), but on the whole they want their members to offer as much content as possible.

Microblog sites place strict limits on the content that can be uploaded, and they find that those limits encourage creativity.

And some microblogging sites are completely hands-off, including Tumblr and WeHeartIt.

A Closer Look at Microblogging

Just as there are many different kinds of social media sites, so also there are many different ways to microblog. One of the most popular ways now actually takes place within the larger social media sites.

When Facebook realized that its members loved the idea of being able to update their followers on what they were doing, it added the status update feature, which sure seems a lot like microblogging. (See Figure 1.5.)

Facebook's system only works within the site, though, so unlike Twitter, which can broadcast your tweets to mobile telephones as well, updates are visible only to friends who happen to be on the site at the time.

For Facebook users, though, it's still very powerful, and Twitter users who want their updates to reach further can use Facebook's Twitter application. This lets them send tweets from within Facebook itself. We use it, and think it's great. You can find it at https://apps.facebook.com/twitter/ or by searching the apps for Twitter.

Facebook isn't the only social media site to add microblogging to its list of features, though. Google Plus and LinkedIn are also social networks targeting specific communities. LinkedIn, for example, is geared toward your professional life, with a system that lets you share status updates just like Facebook, but also lets you create blog posts within your LinkedIn account, as shown in Figure 1.6.

Figure 1.5   Facebook status updates = microblogging.

Figure 1.6   LinkedIn supports blogging, too.

Just as important, the site also lets its users track what people are saying in their posts, what new jobs they get, and much more. And that's just smart business, and social.

YAMMER

Microblogging services thrive most when they ask users to answer a simple question and allow anyone to see the answer. Yammer (www.yammer.com) keeps to those roots but narrows the focus of the question—and the audience, too. (See Figure 1.7.)

Instead of inviting people to share what they're doing (and receiving answers that might range from saving an oil-soaked bird to eating an avocado sandwich), it asks users to explain what they're working on.

But it reveals those answers only to people on the network with the same corporate e-mail address, making it what geeks would call an *intranet* system, which makes it a useful tool for

Figure 1.7 Yammer's restrictions make Twitter look like a free-for-all.

communicating within a business, but not so useful for marketing of any sort.

Introducing . . . Twitter!

And finally, we come to Twitter—the site that has really set the standard in microblogging. Twitter, originally called *twttr,* was founded by programmers Evan Williams, Jack Dorsey, Biz Stone, and Noah Glass in July 2006.

Williams was a serial entrepreneur who had founded a company called Pyra Labs that made project management software. A note-taking feature on that software went on to become Blogger, the free blogging service later bought by Google. In fact, some people credit Williams with coining the word *blogger* to describe people who write Weblogs.

In 2004, Williams left Google to form podcasting company Odeo, and two years later, he created Obvious with Stone, a programmer who had joined Blogger after its acquisition by the search engine giant. The new company bought Odeo, which it later sold to a company called Sonic Mountain. Round and round. It's a game of musical chairs that makes our heads swim, too.

The important thing is that Odeo launched and then began to focus exclusively on a simple chat application called Twitter.

The original idea for Twitter came from Dorsey, an Odeo employee. In an interview for ReadWriteTalk.com Stone described the moment when they first discussed the idea:

> *A few of us were thinking about what are some interesting ways that maybe we can merge SMS [short message service] to the Web," he said. "[Dorsey] had come up with this idea where if you just look at only the status field of an instant message application like AIM, and you just look at that as a sort of really small version of what people are already doing . . . and you just make it super simple, 'Here's what I'm doing.' . . . [W]e kind of went off in a corner and we worked for two weeks and we created a prototype. We showed the rest of the team and everyone just sort of giggled. They all kind of loved it. It was really fun. We used it over the weekend. We found it very compelling and we decided that we would keep working on it.*

That was in March 2006, and initially Twitter was used by the company's employees as a fun form of internal communication. (Tech companies, it seems, might have lava lamps and pinball machines, but they never seem to have watercoolers!)

The service launched officially in October 2006, picked up a South by Southwest (SXSW) Web Award in March 2007, and by April was a hot, up-and-coming social media business, structured as a separate company headed by Dorsey.

Helped by the publicity the SXSW award generated, boosted by references on Blogger (where the company, of course, had good connections), and most important, making itself attractive with an open platform that let other developers extend the service, the site started to take off.

This growth, however, led to some problems. In 2007, Twitter was reported to have had just 98 percent uptime—a loss of three whole days over the year—and tended to suffer particularly badly during major tech conferences (which says something about many of its users, too). (See Figure 1.8.)

It has had some very impressive successes though. Some of the world's leading personalities, corporations, and government bodies are known to use the service, including Barack Obama (@barackobama), former California governor and film star Arnold Schwarzenegger (@schwarzenegger), popular writer Neil Gaiman (@neilhimself), Whole Foods Market (@WholeFoods), and the British Parliament (@UKParliament).

The American Red Cross (@RedCross) and other emergency response organizations, such as the U.S. Federal Emergency

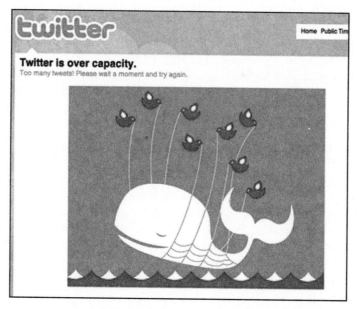

Figure 1.8   Twitter's iconic "fail whale." Designed by Yiying Lu, the beluga whale supported by twittering birds is now a brand in its own right after its frequent appearance on an overstrained Twitter site.

Management Administration (@FEMA), use Twitter as a fast way to communicate information about local disasters.

Two things really distinguish Twitter, though.

The first is its simplicity. Although the service now has piles of additional tools and add-ons, at its core Twitter remains a way of describing what you're doing, thinking, hoping, or dreaming in no more than 140 characters.

That brevity and simplicity have always been key, and they're what brought Twitter its second characteristic: critical mass.

The most difficult moment for any social network is the beginning. It's the chicken and egg problem: People don't want to join a new site until their friends are also online, but those friends are also waiting until their friends join. No one joins precisely because no one's yet joined.

It takes a special push to get a social media site to build a sufficient community for everyone to feel comfortable about climbing on board. For Facebook that came about through it focusing on dating and the social life at Harvard University, and it expanded to other universities only after it already had significant traction in its primary market.

For Twitter it was the boost it received with its SXSW award that had people on the Internet, whether they'd attended SXSW that year in Austin, Texas, or not talking about the service as the next big thing.

As long as it has that critical mass—and with more than 250 million monthly active users, it certainly has that—Twitter is always going to be the microblogging service to beat.

In the next chapter, we'll explain exactly why it's likely to retain its position as the leading microblogging service.

2

Why Is Twitter So Powerful?

Twitter isn't unique.

Yes, it's big and it's got buzz that other sites just don't have.

It's growing at the kind of phenomenal rate that's already forced the social media giants to look over their shoulders and copy some of its best innovations.

Twitter's not the only service that allows people to broadcast short messages. We've already seen that plenty of other sites offer the same service in one form or another, including esoteric services, such as Snapchat.

The difference is that Twitter is by far the most powerful microblogging service available, and it's the one that marketers absolutely need to be including in their online marketing campaigns, large or small.

Twitter and Its Successes

We've mentioned that at its simplest Twitter is just a means to send short updates to people who want to receive them.

The most basic way to do that is to log in to your Twitter account on the Web and type your tweet into the text field. Anyone who looks at your profile can see all of your outgoing tweets. (See Figure 2.1.)

Followers can also see a list of tweets from everyone they follow when they log in to their Twitter home page. They'll also see tweets sent from people they follow to other people they follow, allowing

Figure 2.1 Twitter's new home pages put a big emphasis on search. Your Twitter home page will look a little different.

them to jump into conversations between friends. (What they won't see, though, are tweets sent from someone they're following to someone they're *not* following. That makes it harder to spot new opportunities to make new friends, so it is worth checking out the profiles of the people you're following from time to time to see what conversations you're missing.)

Your Twitter experience then will be made up of sending your own updates and reading tweets from others. And new to the mix, Twitter is occasionally going to intersperse tweets from people it thinks you'll find interesting, so don't be surprised if people you aren't following start to show up. Our suggestion? If they're interesting, follow them.

One of the inspirations for Twitter was the idea of combining Web-based updates with mobile information. Twitter makes it possible for mobile phone users to send and receive updates from their smartphones, whether via text messaging (old school), through a specific Twitter app, or even by having Twitter integrated into the phone's operating system, because Twitter is an integral part of Apple's iOS 8 and beyond.

So if you had just agreed to a joint venture with a marketing partner while attending a conference, and you wanted to share the news right away, you could just pull out your mobile phone and send a quick message to Twitter.

Twitter will then pass that message on to all of your followers, including by broadcasting short message service (SMS) messages to people who have chosen to receive their updates in that fashion.

The benefits of being able to disseminate news so quickly can be huge. The Red Cross has already spotted Twitter's potential and now uses the site to provide updates related to ongoing disasters, along with the Federal Emergency Management Administration, local police departments, fire departments, the National Weather Service, and so many more.

Red Cross volunteers are able to send updates about a new shelter opening or the changing direction of a brushfire and have thousands of people read them at the same time. When brushfires threatened Boulder, Colorado, in 2012, for example, residents relied on Twitter to learn about evacuations, closures, and rescue centers. It was a hugely important service. (See Figure 2.2.)

Twitter also brings the benefit of immediate feedback, which can have tremendous advantages for individuals.

The Power of Twitter's Immediate Feedback

Twitter's speed means that you can send out a tweet from wherever you are and have lots of people read it immediately. It's a service that was originally designed as a fun communications tool but has proved itself to be incredibly valuable as a way of asking for help.

One example: Pastor Carlos Whittaker (@loswhit), service programming director at Buckhead Church in Atlanta, Georgia, found himself stuck at the Dallas airport and was told he would have to wait 6 hours for the next flight. Tired and unhappy at the

Figure 2.2   The American Red Cross's tweets (@RedCross) provide information and disaster-related updates.

thought of spending a night on the airport floor, he sent a tweet about his predicament.

Within just 2 minutes, he had received seven e-mails, three phone calls, and a huge number of tweets.

Best of all, Trevor DeVage of charity group Remedy4ThisHeart turned up and gave Carlos a key to a room at a nearby Hyatt hotel.

That was a helpful response, but sometimes tweets can generate the sort of response that makes an even more important difference to people's lives.

Back in April 2008, for example, James Buck (@jamesbuck), a journalism student at the University of California, Berkeley, was arrested with his interpreter, Mohammed Maree, while photographing an antigovernment rally in Egypt. Sitting in the police van, he was able to use his mobile phone to send the one-word message "arrested" to his followers on Twitter. They immediately alerted the U.S. embassy and his college, which quickly obtained a lawyer for him. Buck continued to provide updates about his arrest via Twitter and was released the following day, which he announced on Twitter with the word *free*.

Both of those examples relied on Twitter followers taking action outside Twitter. But that's not usually where the responses take place.

One of the most enjoyable aspects of Twitter isn't updating friends and family about the small details of your life. That's fun, but it typically works one way.

Twitter is a two-way communication tool, and that's very important.

It means you can ask questions and request help for even very specialized problems and get the expert advice you need, often within seconds of posting the tweet.

Instant Access to Smart People 24/7

Later in this book, we'll talk about how to use Twitter not just as a billboard for making announcements but also as a way of holding conversations with people who matter.

Usually, you'll be holding those conversations with friends or customers. But because Twitter has such a well-educated and professional group of followers, it can also function as a never-closed help center for just about any topic you can imagine.

Look at people's Twitter pages and you'll see this time and time again. (See Figure 2.3.)

Hidden among the announcements about the type of music they're listening to or the work they're doing, you'll see questions about how to fix this problem, where they can buy that gizmo, or even what they should have for supper. (Twitter users do seem to think about food a lot!)

Some of those questions are a bit silly. Some are very technical, but in both cases the smart Twitter community can actually answer them.

The answer to Jerrica's question (in Figure 2.3) about Twitter notifications via e-mail, for example, was "Twitter.com > Account > Settings > Notifications." It took less than 4 minutes to come in.

Figure 2.3 A search for the keyword phrase *anyone know* suggests that a call for help—or at least a call like this—goes out on Twitter several times a minute.

So, that's the history, and that's where Twitter came from. It's an incredibly simple tool that's already had a massive impact on people's lives. Growing out of social media sites to focus on just one tiny action, it's become hugely popular with some of the world's smartest people and highest earners. It's pulled innocents out of prison and given a lost pastor a place to sleep.

It's useful. It's important. And used correctly, it can also generate earnings for any Internet marketer.

But you have to know how to use it. In the rest of this book, we're going to reveal all of the most important tips, strategies, and approaches to getting the most out of Twitter.

It's going to be hands-on, practical, comprehensive, and results driven.

So let's start right at the beginning . . .

3

Getting Started the Right Way on Twitter

A large part of Twitter's beauty is its simplicity. Sign up for many of the other social networking sites, and you'll be asked questions about your life that cover everything ranging from where you went to school to your favorite band or old TV show.

On Twitter, people are happy to let everyone know what they had for lunch (as well as breakfast, supper, brunch, and afternoon snack and what they dunked in their coffee), but that's not because Twitter asks them to.

In fact, the site keeps everything very clean and easy to use.

In this chapter, we're going to help you get to grips with the basics of Twitter. It's not difficult to understand, but you will need to know the way the site works and how to use it. We'll explain what happens during registration, what followers and tweets are, and how to send and receive those all-important messages.

Signing Up—Does Twitter Have the Web's Most Friendly Registration Page?

At some point, all Internet entrepreneurs face a dilemma. They look at Google's home page with its white space and single-line search box, and they realize that simple is good.

Then they look at the list of all the features they want their site to include, and they stuff their home page and their registration page—and every other page—with features and information that only a fraction of their users will want and only a few people will ever use.

It's just too tempting, and it's a mistake that gums up the works of businesses as varied as dating services and networking sites.

Twitter didn't make that mistake. Hit the *Sign up* link on its home page, and you'll be taken to a sign-up page that has just four fields: name, username, password, and e-mail address. (See Figure 3.1.)

It couldn't be simpler, could it?

Well, actually, this is where simple can be bad.

It's the first place you can make a mistake.

Twitter asks for two names because those names appear in different places and in different ways.

Your full name will appear on the right side of the page, above your mini bio. It will also be used to identify your tweets on some third-party clients, such as TweetDeck, or the standalone Twitter apps.

Your username, though, isn't just a phrase you're going to enter when you sign in. It will form part of your uniform resource

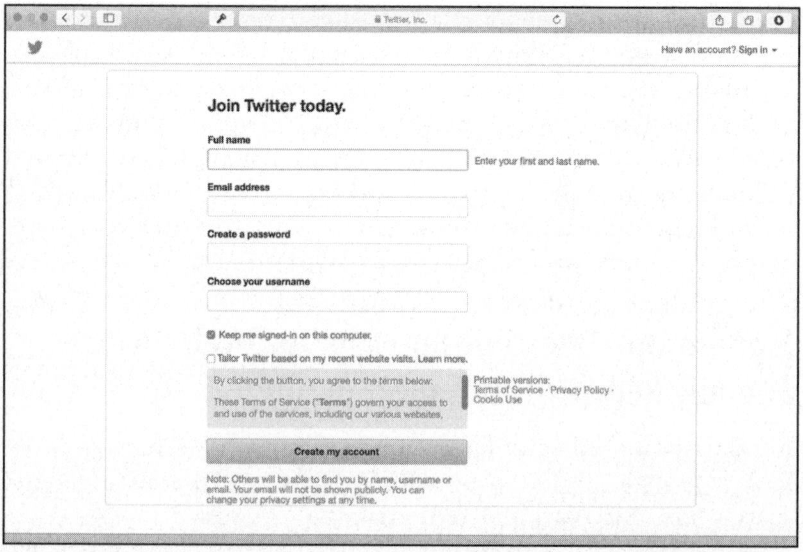

Figure 3.1   Join the conversation, but introduce yourself first.

locator (URL) and will be visible whenever you promote your Twitter page. In many ways, it's your identity in the Twitterverse.

It's like a choosing a domain name for a website or even a business name. Choose your Twitter handle or name poorly, and you could adversely affect your ability to gather followers and build a reputation. If people who know you can't find you on Twitter because they can't figure out your username, you'll be missing opportunities. If your username is silly or slang, it'll adversely affect your ability to be professional, too, or vice versa.

Your username might be one of the first things you enter, but it should be an item you think about carefully.

Your full name is often a possible Twitter handle (as it is for Dave—@DaveTaylor—and Joel—@JoelComm), provided it hasn't been taken already and provided you can squeeze it into the space available (you've got just 15 characters). Another good option is to use your website's domain name if that's clear and meaningful to potential customers. That would link your site with your Twitter account and make it clear that the one is just a natural extension of the other.

Whatever you choose, just make sure that it's:

1. **Closely associated with you**

   The formula "twitter.com/username" makes finding people on Twitter very easy. If you don't want to search around for someone, you can just pop his or her name after *twitter.com* and see if the person is there. (Usually, when writing about Twitterers, the *twitter.com/* is replaced with @.)

   It's very simple, and it means you can have hours of (almost) endless fun. Try surfing to twitter.com/billgates, for example, or twitter.com/richardbranson. Or toss in any other celebrity you can think of, and try to spot which Twitterers are real stars.

Tip: For well-known celebrities, Twitter often has a *verified user* check mark adjacent to their account name. It's not doing this as much as it used to, however, so that might be phasing out.

People are going to be able to use this easy URL facility to find you only if your username is a word or phrase that's closely associated with you or your brand.

For example, if you wanted to guess whether Starbucks is on Twitter, you'd try twitter.com/starbucks, and you'd score, as shown in Figure 3.2.

Figure 3.3, by contrast, demonstrates that when the Luxor Hotel and Casino of Las Vegas jumped on Twitter, someone else already had *luxor*, so it ended up with @LuxorLV. Still good, still memorable, but not quite as optimal as it would have been without the *LV* suffix.

That's made even more important by Twitter's on-site search engine, which is very precise. Although Facebook, Google Plus, and even LinkedIn's search engines will return suggestions and near misses if it can't find an exact match, Twitter will just tell you that it can't find the person you're looking for.

Figure 3.2   It's easy to guess @Starbucks.

Figure 3.3   The Luxor Hotel and Casino, Las Vegas. Unfortunately, someone already had @Luxor, so it's relegated to the somewhat less preferable @LuxorLV.

If you've picked a random username, you've left a valuable advantage on the table. Don't do it! In fact, you can apply the radio test: if you were on the radio and told people, "Find me on Twitter as..." would you then need to spell out or otherwise explain your Twitter name, or would it be immediately obvious, as it is for both Joel and Dave?

2. **Easy to remember**

If a username is closely associated with you, it should be easy to remember, but that isn't always the case. Sometimes your optimal handle is already taken, especially if you wanted something such as just your first or last name.

Opt for a long name to make it stand out, and you'll increase the chances that even a small typo will send potential followers the wrong way.

Tossing in numbers as a way of keeping a version of a common name to yourself works fine in passwords, but as a username that's going to form part of your URL, it's a strict no-no. So @Joel33 or @Dave303 really isn't a very good handle at all.

Keep it short, simple to remember, and closely associated with who you are, what you do, or what your business delivers to your customers.

You can change your Twitter name after you've signed up, if you really must, but if you're going to do that, do so as quickly as possible after you sign up. Switching to a new name after you've already created a long list of followers may confuse people and mean they won't be able to communicate with you easily or engage in that precious dialog. Although you'll keep your followers, you'll also lose the old conversations that will be visible only on your old account. It's something you should really try to avoid.

Twitter works best when the account feels personal, so in general the best bet is to *put your real full name in the first field and use either your name or the name of your business as your username.*

Who's on Twitter? Your First Followers!

Once you've entered your name, picked a username, and chosen a password, you'll begin a five-step process that will start you following people on Twitter.

None of these steps takes more than a minute or two, but the good news is you can skip them if you want to.

The even better news is that you *should* skip one of these steps—at least for now.

The first thing Twitter offers is to have you automatically follow popular Twitter accounts as a way to ensure you don't start out with an empty feed. You can pick specific categories or just let it show you who's popular at that moment, as shown in Figure 3.4.

Starting with Twitter superstars, such as Ellen DeGeneres, Justin Timberlake, Jimmy Fallon, and President Barak Obama, is

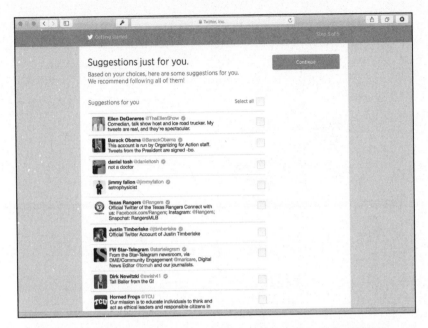

Figure 3.4 Some Twitter users start by following popular Twitter accounts.

smart. Agree with their politics or not, it's educational to see how they're using the service.

The next request Twitter will make, the one we're leery of, is to search any online mail service that you use—such as Gmail, Hotmail, AOL, and Outlook—to see whether anyone with an e-mail address listed in your address book has already registered an account at Twitter. (See Figure 3.5.)

Clearly, this capability is going to be very, very helpful.

It means that you can start following your friends and contacts right away. And it means that you can bring in everyone you know so that they're following you.

So why do we think you should skip this stage when you sign up?

Because the most powerful way to win followers on Twitter is to follow them yourself.

If you start following people on Twitter, they'll receive a message saying that you're following them.

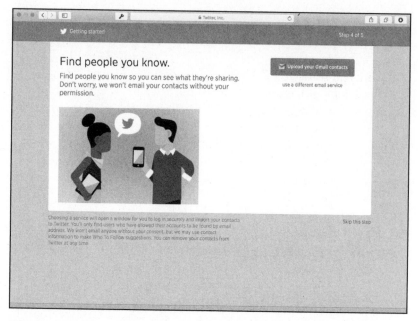

Figure 3.5 You can start searching on Twitter for your Gmail contacts before you've created your profile, but we recommend you set up your own account first.

They'll then come to your Twitter page, and at this stage of your registration, what will they see?

Not much at all. In fact, you'll look like a spammer.

You haven't uploaded a picture yet. You haven't designed your Twitter page yet. You have no color scheme, no theme, nothing.

You haven't even issued a tweet yet!

Why would anyone choose to follow a Twitterer with a profile like that?

Being able to see which of your friends and contacts are already on Twitter—and follow them right away—is such a valuable tool that you shouldn't waste it on an empty Twitter page. Wait until your own profile is ready.

Until then, following your friends and contacts is going to be more valuable for Twitter, which will pick up referrals to everyone on your contact list, than it will be to you.

Don't worry; you will be able to come back to this step later when your profile is ready, so our advice would be to skip this step for now.

And you're done! Congrats and welcome to Twitter.

Now let's go back and talk about those celebrity Twitter accounts for a minute, because although we like the idea of you studying celebrity tweets, there's also a significant downside: you'll be discovering what Twitter is all about soon enough anyway, and these Twitterers—with their millions of followers—are not going to follow you back.

Your profile will show that you're following lots of people but that no one is following you.

Ideally, you want your Twitter profile to have more followers than the number of people you're following. We'll spend a lot of time explaining why that's important later in the book, but for now just understand that when you follow many more people than are following you, you look like the forever alone guy in desperate search of a party. When more people are following you than you're following, *you* are the party.

We like to look at it as a ratio, followers:following. Joel has a ratio with @JoelComm of 80:1, and Dave's @DaveTaylor account has a ratio of 14:1. If your ratio is near 1:1, or even lower, you need followers!

When you start out on Twitter, you're always going to be following more people than are following you, so at this stage, it's not a huge issue. Don't follow everyone that Twitter throws at you during registration, but if you see someone who looks interesting, feel free to add him or her.

We'll fix that ratio thing as you start to gain followers of your own further along in the process.

Create an Inviting Twitter Profile

Skip past the instant searching and follow suggestions, and you'll be taken right into your Twitter page. (See Figure 3.6.)

At this stage, there won't be much to see.

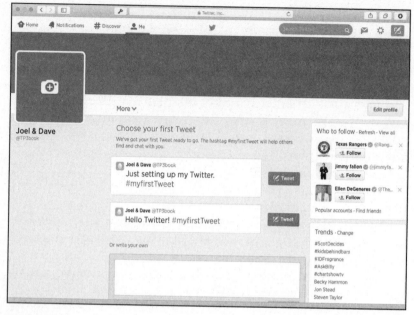

Figure 3.6   A brand-new Twitter profile. Think of it as a blank canvas on which you're about to create a marketing masterpiece, and start at the very top, not the bottom.

You'll have the default blue background. Your profile image will consist of the default blue square with the camera icon. And you'll have no followers, you'll be following no one, and you'll have no updates.

This, though, isn't the page that your followers will see when they stop by to read your tweets. You can see that page by clicking the link *Home* on the very top left. Once you're up and running on Twitter, it will show all of the tweets you've posted. Anyone can see this page by surfing to twitter.com/[your username] or by clicking on a link to your username anywhere on Twitter. That's what's shown in Figure 3.7.

Those tweets will also be visible on this page—your Twitter home page—but they'll be surrounded by the tweets the people you've chosen to follow posted. This is your reading page. It's the page you see when you open Twitter. Only you get to see it, and it

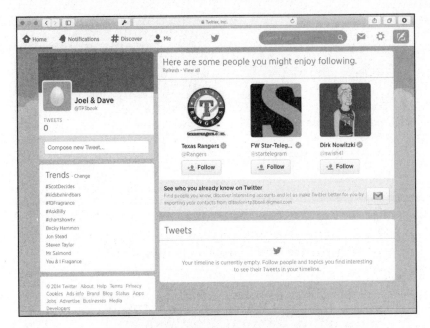

Figure 3.7 What everyone else sees for a brand-new Twitter account. Boring and unlikely to inspire people to follow you back!

will be unique because only you will have chosen to follow that particular mixture of Twitterers.

There are a number of links on this page that you need to be familiar with. The most important are *Tweets, Followers,* and *Following,* all on the left. Any list of Twitter users is shown as a set of what look like mini digital business cards. See Figure 3.8 for what we mean.

In fact, click on the little gear icon adjacent to a Twitter user's account name, and a variety of options appear, as shown in Figure 3.9.

In terms of actual Tweets, if you mention another Twitterer by username, the tweet automatically links to his or her Twitter account. That shortens the number of remaining characters you have available for the rest of your message, but the person you mention will be able to see that tweet and respond to you. You don't have to push the link on your following list to do this.

Figure 3.8 Profile minicards also show you whether you follow those users. If you don't, click on *Follow* to follow them.

Figure 3.9 Lots of options for how to interact with the Twitter account from the options menu. In this instance, the account is @AbsoluteLoJack.

Pressing the reply link on one of his or her tweets does exactly the same thing, and so does manually writing the username into your tweet. Just make sure you include the @ prefix.

You can also send a direct message (DM) to someone you're following—but only if he or she is also following you. These secret communications are stored in a private inbox and can be read only by the recipient. In the early days of Twitter, DMs were an easy way to have a quick one-to-one private conversation, but now if you follow the wrong people, you might find yourself drowning in pesky automated messages and spam. Keep an eye on it; sometimes these messages are good, and other times they're just worthless.

You can also choose to unfollow someone whom you're following, which removes him or her from your list, and to block someone, which removes you from his or her list. Your tweets will no longer appear on his or her Twitter page, and the only way the person can read what you're writing is to go directly to your timeline.

Blocking can be useful if you're being harassed or stalked by someone, but mostly you'll find yourself using it to block the porn bots that crop up on your follower list every now and then.

> Remember that Twitter has an asymmetrical follow system unlike a service such as Facebook: on Facebook you can't friend Dave without him friending you, too, but on Twitter you can follow Dave independent of whether he follows you.

Clicking to see your list of followers—the people who have chosen to follow your tweets—will reveal largely the same options.

You'll be able to mention a follower in your tweet, send a direct message, and block him or her. The list will also indicate whether you're already following someone following you, and if you're not following him or her, it will provide a way to do so.

There are four links along the very top of the page. *Home* takes you back to your Twitter home page, but it's the next link,

Notifications, that's very important. In fact, you should find yourself clicking it frequently—*at least once a day.*

This link shows all of the tweets that have mentioned your username. Usually those will consist of public messages deliberately aimed at you. They may also be tweets that talk about you. Either way, you'll want to see them and likely reply to them in return.

That link—and it's likely to be the one you use most on Twitter—is followed by the *Discover* link if you want to explore and the *Me* link if you want to see how others view your profile.

On the right side of the top navigational bar are a search box, link to your inbox (DMs), settings and preferences menu, and a *New Tweet* button.

Worth highlighting is that the link to tweets that mention your username won't reveal who's talking about your product or your industry, your real name, or any other keyword phrase you might want to track on Twitter. It just tracks your username. You can enter other keyword phrases in the search box, and—very helpfully—you can save those searches, too, making it very easy to follow what other Twitterers are saying about the topics most important to you. When Twitter rolls out its geolocation service, you'll even be able to restrict those searches to people in your area, allowing you to target a local market. Those saved searches will appear in a list below the search box.

Finally, on just about every page you can see a list of trends, subjects or hashtags (we'll explain those in a bit) that are currently the most popular on Twitter.

Of course, all of these lists will start to fill only when you begin tweeting and using Twitter.

That's what we're going to do now.

At the top of your home page is a sample of two starting tweets, followed by the standard Twitter box in which you can make your first tweet. (See Figure 3.10.)

Hold up just a second. You may be ready to jump right in and begin tweeting right away, but that may not be the best way to start out.

Let's face it; with thousands of other people just dipping their toes in the water, it's a sure bet that the people at Twitter aren't going to read every first tweet sent by every new Twitterer.

Figure 3.10   Is your first tweet ready to send?

And your followers aren't interested in this first tweet yet because, well, you don't have any! Sending a tweet at this stage won't do you any harm, but it won't do you any good either. No one will read it.

Or at least no people will read it until they've started following you. At that time, they'll be free to see every tweet you've ever sent, which might not be very interesting at all.

It's a bit like that first blog post if you're a blogger. A post with the content "My first post" not only is uninteresting, but also is senseless to leave up forever.

(And in case you were wondering, Joel's first tweet back in May 2007 was "Checking out twitter for the first time." Dave's first tweet, just a few months later in November 2007, was "blogging about twitter, ingeniously enough.:)" You can see both tweets, and lots of others, at www.myfirsttweet.com.)

So, forget about sending tweets for now.

Don't worry about finding some friends to follow.

And you certainly don't need to concern yourself about turning on your mobile to update your friends while you're on the go.

In just a moment, we're going to take a step back and provide you a high-level philosophical approach to Twitter (and social media in general) that many of the biggest brands have yet to understand. Trust us when we say you will find it revolutionary.

But for the moment, let's click the *Settings* link at the top of the page and give yourself a proper profile.

You'll be presented a ton of options, mostly accessible from the menu on the left side of the screen. The options there are Account, Security and privacy, Password, Mobile, E-mail notifications, Web notifications, Profile, Design, Apps, and Widgets.

For each of these options, there are a variety of boxes and fields to fill out, as shown with the Account settings in Figure 3.11.

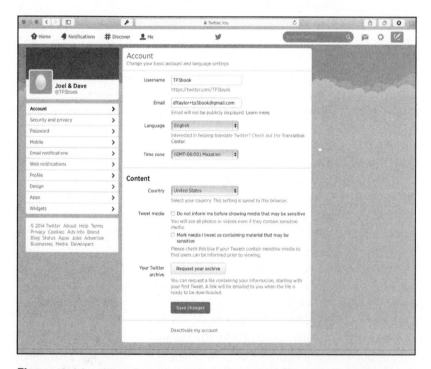

Figure 3.11 What Twitter calls *settings* actually offers a lot more than technical choices. It's one of the most important pages for successful Twitter marketing.

USERNAME

That starts with asking what your name is.

Yes, you should know your name, and that question shouldn't be hard. But it might be.

You probably have more than one name. You have a name. Your website might have a name. Your business might have a completely different name.

And that's assuming you just have one business and one website.

We've already pointed out the importance of choosing a username that can be typed directly into the browser. That's vital, and even though it's going to appear at the top of your profile page, it's never going to be pretty.

Because it's also a URL, whatever phrase you choose is going to appear as one word.

Your name will appear on the right of your Twitter page and will reveal who you *really* are.

So before you type in your username, *you have to decide which brand you want your Twitter page to represent.*

Will the tweets be about what *you're* doing now, or will they be about what your company or your website is doing now?

Do you see the difference?

It's a vital one, and it will help to determine who follows you, what they're looking for, and what sort of community you're going to build.

The username you choose is as important as the domain name for a website. It tells readers what to expect.

Dave has two Twitter accounts, for example. One is @FilmBuzz and it's for people who want to keep up with what's going on in the film industry and try their luck with the occasional film trivial question. They don't know Dave by name, so the descriptive name makes a lot more sense.

Dave also has a personal Twitter profile, @DaveTaylor, that uses both his username and real name so that he's easy to find and so that anyone reading his tweets understands that they're coming directly from him. Joel, with @JoelComm, obviously has the same strategy.

In both of the latter cases, followers are getting information that they can trust from well-known industry experts.

Bear in mind that if you do want to create more than one Twitter ID, you will need to use a different e-mail address on each account. That can be a problem if you have only a small number of addresses, so here's a handy workaround: create a Gmail account and you can place a period in any part of the address to create what Twitter sees as a new address. In other words, to Gmail, john.doe@gmail.com and j.ohndoe@gmail.com are the same address and are going to have their mail delivered to the same mailbox. To Twitter, however, those are different addresses, allowing you to use the same Gmail address on multiple accounts.

There's another handy Gmail tip you can use, too, if you'd prefer: you can add + followed by any sequence of characters, and Gmail is smart enough to know that it should be delivering to the prefix only. In other words, johndoe@gmail.com and johndoe+twitter@gmail.com are functionally identical. We use this all the time to tag where we've submitted our e-mail address online!

You can change your username without affecting the tweets and messages you've already sent and received, and without losing a single follower.

That doesn't mean you should just enter the first username you think of, however!

Although your current store of messages will be safe, you will still want to tell your followers about the change. When you've got a lot of followers—and by using the strategies in the next chapter you *will* have a lot of followers—that's always going to be a real pain.

In fact, one good strategy when you join Twitter is to open multiple accounts so that you can tweet about different subjects. Twitter doesn't allow cybersquatting—and Twitterers who have tried it have had their accounts suspended—but if you think you might need more than one account, then it's worth grabbing your usernames sooner rather than later.

E-MAIL

Your choice of name and username isn't going to be too difficult. If you have more than one identity or brand, it might take a little thought. But usually the choice should be clear, and you can always create more than one account. You'll need to use a separate e-mail account for each timeline, so the only limit will be the number of e-mail accounts you can rustle up.

That means your choice of e-mail is a lot easier.

This isn't an e-mail address that anyone is going to see.

If people want to contact you through Twitter, they'll have to do it either by replying to one of your tweets or by sending you a direct message.

But they won't see your e-mail address.

The address you enter here will be used only to receive information such as Twitter's newsletters, to receive notifications if you have that enabled, and to change your password.

If you're the kind of person who tends to forget passwords, that last use case can be helpful! Make sure then that you choose an e-mail address that you actually use.

TIME ZONE

Time on the Internet tends to be a strange thing. Check your e-mail client and you might find all sorts of strange times attached to the e-mails you've received; often they look like they have no relationship at all to the time the message was sent.

Usually, that doesn't matter at all.

On Twitter, though, because tweets describe what you're doing *now*, time is important. (See Figure 3.12.)

So, for the most recent posts, Twitter displays how long ago the tweets were sent. If a tweet is a day old, though, the time stamp refers to the time the tweet was sent based on the time zone *the follower* entered on the settings page.

Which can end up being a bit confusing. We'd rather know what time of day the person sent his or her tweets according to *our* time zone.

Figure 3.12 Three different kinds of time stamps on my tweets as seen by a follower. Only one of them was right, but at least they're in the right order—and that's what counts!

Which time zone to use is not a hard question, but this is one that Twitter got wrong.

Building Out Your Profile

The next series of steps are associated with the *Profile* option on the left, as shown in Figure 3.13. Click *Profile* to move to this area so that you can continue.

NAME

The first two fields in the profile area are photos, one that's your portrait photo (because it's unlikely you look like an egg) and the other that's your profile page header. We'll talk about both of those shortly, so let's stay focused on the text and informational fields right now.

Figure 3.13 Options on your Profile page.

The first important field to consider is *Name*. If your account is a personal account, this is easy: it's your name. No rocket science there. Joel has "Joel Comm" as his name, for example.

But what if it's a brand, a product name, an acronym, or even some hipster slang? What does @Starbucks have? "Starbucks Coffee." @USPS? "U.S. Postal Service." How about @TheRock? That's a celebrity, actually, and "The Rock" is his nickname. Don't know? Dwayne Johnson. He has a rather impressive 7.4 million followers, and he follows—ready for this?—one person: @MuhammadAli.

Sometimes names are not well thought through, even with big brands. For example, @FEMA is the Federal Emergency Management Administration, but its name field is simply "FEMA." Not so useful.

The long and short of it is that just as you need to spend time thinking about your shortened username on Twitter, the

@[something] that you register, you should also spend time considering your name. If you have a common name, you might be "The Dave Taylor" or "The Real Joel," but it's just so much more important if you're a brand, product, or company.

And here's the tough part: there aren't many letters available, so if you want to list "The University of Saskatchewan, Department of Computer Science," you're out of luck. Maybe "U of S, Dept of CompSci."

You can tweak and fiddle with this as much as you'd like without confusion, and once someone's following you on Twitter, odds are he or she won't see it very often anyway. (But flip back about a dozen pages: the minibusiness cards show both the Twitter username and the name for each person.)

Location

Twitter asks, "Where in the world are you?"

Sometimes, changing your location to reflect where you happen to be working on a particular project can be very helpful. Usually, though, you'll be working in the same place most of the time, so you should be a little careful here.

Joel doesn't try to hide the fact that he lives in Denver, Colorado. But his products have nothing to do with his geographic location. When he attends conferences, he meets people from around the country, and his books, courses, and products are read and used by people around the world.

As a result, although he doesn't think that placing his location on his Twitter bio would really affect his branding, he doesn't want people to feel that his work is somehow connected to Colorado or is just for residents of the state. So he omits it in his profile.

Dave includes his hometown of Boulder, Colorado, in his profile both because he's a proud resident of the tourist-destination city and because being a Boulder resident is part of his personal branding.

If there's a chance that your location could adversely affect or localize your work, then you might want to leave the location off, too. Otherwise city and state or even just city name is fine.

WEBSITE

And now we come to something that's crucial.

Twitter's profile structure provides space for you to promote just one website for each account. In fact, as we'll point out later in this section, with a little creativity it's possible to promote all the websites you want.

But even then, one website—the link that appears beneath your name on the screen—will always be the most prominent.

It's the one that people will click to find out exactly who you are and what lies behind you as a Twitterer.

That makes the link very, very powerful.

Usually, you'll want to link to your main website. Sometimes, though, you might want to change this link to suit a particular promotion. If you were promoting a new product, e-book, or affiliate product, for example, you could tweet about it and link from your profile to a specific, related landing page rather than the site's home page.

Your tweets then would become another channel to bring potential buyers to your store.

Do you see how useful this can be?

Warning: don't put a shortened URL in this space. Because Twitter leaves such a small amount of room in the status box, you will need to use shortened links in your tweets. But you want the full address in your profile page. That should help generate curiosity, and even if it doesn't generate a click right away, it will increase name recognition for your website.

Generally, we subscribe to the idea that your blog is your home, not just your home page. It is the only place on the Web where you ultimately have complete control over content.

Although we are huge fans of social media, remember that we are participants of a community. That community is owned by other companies, each of which is concerned with bringing value to its members, and to its bottom line. Twitter, Facebook, YouTube, Google Plus, Instagram, Pinterest, and the multitude of other social sites are running a business, with the goal of being profitable.

That means terms of service for any of these sites can change at any time if the company deems it necessary to increase profitability.

We've seen brands work diligently to build their social media follower base only to discover that a change in a site's terms of service has made it more challenging to actually reach those followers.

We don't say this to frighten you in any way. It is essential that businesses and brands leverage the power of Twitter and other social sites. But being aware of which sites you have control over and which you do not is important in the big scheme of things. Just remember that a key point of your engagement is to build a relationship with your prospects and customers so that the relationship can persist beyond the social sites. So be sure to have an interesting, informative, and engaging website or blog, so people can continue the dialog with you on your own turf!

Bio

So far, all of the fields we've discussed have been very, very simple.

They're very important—and you should know that they're much more important than they look—but none of them should have you scratching your head for more than a few seconds.

Your bio will take some effort and a fair bit of thought, though.

Writing about yourself is never much fun. That's especially true when you're doing it for business. You have to find the things in your life that are interesting to others, make yourself appear professional, and do both without boasting or sounding vain.

Usually, that's pretty hard. But Twitter makes it a *real* challenge: it gives you only 160 characters.

That's right; you get just 20 more characters than you have to write a tweet to describe your entire life history.

What a relief!

That means you can't go into detail and talk about all the things you've done and what you do for others. All you can do is choose one or two of the most important facts about you and write a sentence. (See Figure 3.14.)

Figure 3.14 Dave's bio as it appears on Twitter. Notice he includes his location and site URL, too.

For a long time, Joel's tongue-in-cheek bio used to say:

Astronaut. Nuclear Physicist. Brain Surgeon. You know, the usual stuff.

That's a very simple structure to follow, and you could use exactly the same model or produce your own. If you publish a sports website, for example, you could write something like:

Football fan, youth coach, and all-around sports nut with dodgy knees.

The format is three one- or two-word phrases that describe who you are or what you do, followed by a short joke to finish it off.

If you wanted to create a bio like this, you don't have to do any more than fill in these blanks:

[Professional description 1], [professional description 2], and [professional description 3] who likes to [personal description].

A professional photographer looking to use Twitter to promote his or her services could easily use that format to create a bio that said:

Wedding photographer, portrait pro, and creative artist who likes to photograph his kids at embarrassing moments.

A landscape contractor could come up with a bio that said:

Tree surgeon, garden expert, and green-fingered designer who likes to smell freshly cut grass.

And someone who blogs about sports could use that format to create this bio:

Lakers fan, Mets nut, and fantasy football coach who likes to tailgate downwind of the barbeques.

Do you see how bios like these leave room for just two or three basic facts about you while allowing space for a little personal touch? That's all you have room for on Twitter, and it's all you need. It's a strategy that many people on the site have chosen to follow and for good reason: it's easy and it works.

If people want to find out more, they can always come to your website. (We told you that link was going to be important!)

So, one way of writing your Twitter bio is to summarize yourself in 160 characters. That's the approach both of us have chosen, and it's a very simple one.

An alternative approach is to write a bio that discusses a particular project.

This is a very different use of Twitter. Instead of tweeting about you in general, you'll be tweeting on one theme, which you can then change when that project ends.

British comedy actor and writer Stephen Fry (@stephenfry), for example, is known for being tech savvy. He has a website that he updates frequently and on which he blogs, vlogs, and podcasts. He also tweets several times a day, even when he's working.

He probably does that mostly because he enjoys it—tweeting is fun, after all—but there's no question that his tweets also help generate interest in his latest projects so that when they're released, they already have an audience.

When the British Broadcasting Company (BBC) sent Fry around the world to film a documentary about endangered animals, for example, he constantly changed his location on Twitter to reflect his location and updated his bio to describe what he was doing at the time.

His tweets still helped promote his personal brand. They were still about what he was doing at the time (and yes, that included descriptions of what he was eating for breakfast at the hotel). *But because the bio placed them in the context of a large project, those tweets were easier for new followers to understand, and they had a very strong promotional effect.*

This is something that any marketer could do.

A photographer sent to Alaska for a week to shoot oil wells could change the location to reflect where he or she is now and alter his or her bio:

Currently shooting oil wells in Alaska for British Petroleum.

A landscape contractor could edit his or her bio to describe a big project he or she has been hired to complete:

Now designing the flower beds for Ventura's new Ben Sheffer Park.

And someone who was writing an e-book about fantasy football could write this in his or her bio:

Now working on the ultimate guide to real success with fantasy football.

Tweets describe what you're doing at one particular moment. They can't describe what you're doing over a period that lasts days, weeks, or months. Your bio can do that, and when it does, it focuses your tweets on that one project.

When you have a lot of followers, it can also be a very powerful way of promoting your work.

CONNECT TO FACEBOOK

Another big question to answer is whether you want to tie your Facebook identity to your Twitter account. There are good arguments both for and against this practice. The biggest issue is that most people use Facebook for mostly personal promotion, sometimes with a smattering of professional promotion.

If you're using Twitter mostly for professional updates, for promoting a product or service, for promoting your consulting availability, or for similar activities, then there's a disconnect between your personal Facebook account and your professional Twitter account. In that case, don't connect them.

Twitter also suggests in its wording that you connect a Twitter account to a specific business page or fan page on Facebook. But we've never seen that work, so it's best to assume it's not an option. (Furthermore, with the speed at which Facebook changes features, this option could be gone by the time we're done writing this paragraph, or it could be completely redesigned and work very differently.)

PHOTO

While we're in the *Profile* section, let's look at the two photos associated with your Twitter profile.

We both believe that you should first prepare your page before you start sending and receiving tweets. Once you've completed your bio (and yes, you can change it later if you're not completely satisfied with it), your next step should be to upload a picture.

You need to upload a picture to your Twitter profile.

There's no getting around this step.

If you don't add a photo to your profile, you'll appear on the page as a grey egg against an orange background. That's not very attractive, and worst of all, it makes you look like you're not serious about your customers on Twitter.

When people have added their photo, they'll expect to see yours in return.

It has to be a good picture, too, one that portrays you as both professional and personable—exactly what your tweets should do.

Remember, though, that the picture itself is going to appear very small. Although the image is clickable and can be seen in full size, few people bother. So it's a good idea to use a close-up of your face that makes you recognizable, even when you're no bigger than a thumbnail. Try to include a full-body shot, and your head will appear no larger than a couple of pixels wide on someone's screen.

You'll usually be better off with a good portrait that shows you smiling and at ease.

That's easier said than done, and in practice people make a lot of mistakes here.

Spend any time at all on social networking sites, and you'll see photograph after photograph that looks blurry or unfocused or is just plain inappropriate. Here are a number of guidelines to follow when adding your picture to any social media site, including Twitter:

♦ Don't hold the camera yourself.

Showing your arm doesn't look cool. In fact, it looks like you couldn't find a friend to hold the camera for you, or you don't know how to work the camera's self-timer. Neither of those creates good impressions—and neither creates good pictures either. Selfies are fun, but not in this context.

Both of us have hired professional photographers for our social media head shots and portraits. If you're serious about marketing with social media, that's something you might want to consider, too. You can either visit a local photography studio or ask your friends and colleagues for a recommendation. Expect to pay between $99 and $200.

Alternatively, you can just ask someone to lend you a hand so that you don't have to show your arm.

♦ Use a good camera.

Many laptops today come with built-in webcams. Desktop Web cameras are as common as a keyboard and mouse, and even the cheapest mobile phone comes complete with a lens, a flash, and enough software to run a portable photography studio.

But don't use them.

Cameras like these tend to produce lower-quality images that have lots of distortion. They're hard to focus and they often produce images that are grainy rather than clear.

If you want to video conference with a friend or a business partner on the other side of the country, your webcam will do a fine job.

If you want to snap your friends at a birthday dinner, your smartphone is just the ticket.

But when you're creating a portrait that will represent you on a social media site, use a real camera. Nothing else is good enough.

♦ Keep the backgrounds to a minimum.

Because you have such a tiny amount of space for your portrait, anything in the background is going to interfere with the most important item in the frame: you.

Ideally, your features should fill most of the frame. And behind you there should be almost nothing.

You might be able to get away with a horizon line, the sea or the sky, but if the background is busy in any way—if it shows trees, parts of buildings, or your car—it's going to distract from your portrait and look unfocused.

Find a nice white wall or a good high balcony, and stand your friend, with the camera, directly in front of you.

♦ Show yourself.

And finally, use *your* picture, not a photograph of your cat, your dog, your hamster, your favorite comic book hero, or some squiggle that you feel might do a good job of representing you.

If you're tweeting on behalf of your company, the company may require that you use your company logo. However, we recommend that the profile photo be of the person who is managing the account. Customers are far more likely to connect with a brand that has a human face than with a brand that has a sterile, impersonal logo.

Social media is all about personal branding. It's about the connections you build as an individual and how you work that network.

To create those connections, you can't be a wallflower. You need to show your face. So shy or not, you need to upload a picture to your profile.

And it has to be a good one!

Checking Out Security and Privacy

There are lots and lots of other options in the settings area of your new Twitter account, but we want to mention two specific things before we move on to the next topic, both of which are in *Security and privacy*.

The first is login verification and it's to do with keeping your account safe from hackers and other people who might try to steal your password and break in, and the second is about Tweet privacy. (See Figure 3.15.)

Login Verification

You might initially shy away from the idea of giving Twitter your cell phone number, but every day there are more stories of passwords being stolen en masse from online services, something that can affect users with even the most complicated passwords.

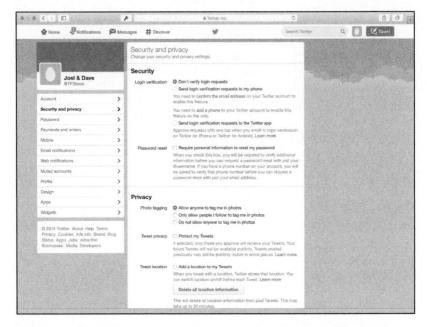

Figure 3.15   Security and privacy are both important to tweak!

Login verification solves that. Every time you go to log in to your Twitter account, you'll enter your username and password, but then the service will send a secret temporary security code—such as 241439—to your registered phone number (so make sure it's able to receive text messages!). You'll need to enter that to gain access to your Twitter account.

The benefit? Huge. Thieves can steal your password, and unless they also steal your phone, they still can't get into your account.

Just do it. In fact, two-factor or two-step verification is a smart thing to do everywhere you can, including your Facebook and Gmail accounts.

TWEET PRIVACY

Twitter has the capability of keeping all your tweets confidential so that only the people you follow can see them, instead of the default of letting everyone in the world see them.

If you're using Twitter for marketing, do not choose this option!

You want to let anyone see your tweets who wants to. You want as many people as possible to come to your Twitter page; realize that you have fantastic, interesting tweets that they want to read; and sign up to be your followers.

If people can't see your updates, they're not going to sign up. You'll be restricted to tweeting to the friends, family, and contacts whom you've chosen.

That's the digital equivalent of a store owner hanging a *closed* sign on the door and dealing only with his or her friends. In other words, it makes your social media presence antisocial.

If you want to tweet only about personal stuff, that's fine. But that's a very different use of Twitter. If you want to use Twitter to build your brand and grow your business, then leave that box unchecked.

Notifications to Notice

Ready to start tweeting? Not quite, there are just a couple of additional things to set before we unleash you on the Twitterverse!

The first is to set your e-mail and Web notifications.

These let you choose how often you want Twitter to bother you.

If you let it, Twitter will bother you a lot. You want it to bother you sometimes and in ways that help you build followers and enhance the site's marketing power.

When Twitter started, one of the options related to @replies. This setting determined whether other people's responses to the tweets they read appeared in your timeline, and if so, which people's. You could choose among showing everyone's replies, showing only replies sent among people you're following, and showing no replies at all.

That's no longer the case. In a controversial decision, the people at Twitter decided that the only replies that you'll see are those among people you're already following.

So if you're following Joel's tweets, and he sends an @reply tweet to someone else you're following, you'll see that message when you log in to Twitter. But if he replies to someone you're *not* following, you can see that message only by looking closely at his timeline.

That's both good news and bad news.

The bad news is that you'll be missing opportunities to make new contacts. The benefit of Twitter is that you're able to connect with other people in your industry. And the best way to see who on Twitter is in your industry is by following the conversations and looking at who is talking to whom. If all you do is read the tweets that reach your Twitter page, you're going to be missing lots of chats you could join and contacts you could make.

That's why there's also good news. It means that to get the most out of Twitter, it's no longer enough to read the tweets that the site pushes to your Twitter page. You also have to read the tweets on Twitterers' timelines. And when people come to your timeline to see whom you're talking to, they'll see your bio, your background, and your link.

Limiting the @replies option might have reduced networking opportunities but it's improved your marketing power.

In fact, there are quite a few different Twitter actions you can receive notifications about in your e-mail, as shown in Figure 3.16.

You should also choose to receive e-mails when you pick up a new follower and when someone sends you a direct message—at least initially. (To get to that setting, you'll need to scroll down from the top part of the *E-mail notifications* screen shown in Figure 3.16.)

As you're building your follower list, you'll want to see who's joining your community. But once your community really starts to take off, and you're getting dozens of new followers a day, those e-mails will get a bit annoying and will stop being useful.

The same is true of direct messages. Because so many people use them as autoresponders, thanking others for following them, your inbox will quickly look like a spam folder. And with no search or filtering, it's impossible to find an important message should you receive one. Keep the notification on at the beginning just so that you can see how direct messaging works, but as soon as it starts to overrun with spam—if it does—then go ahead and turn it off, too.

Figure 3.16   *E-mail notifications* settings in Twitter.

Tweeting with Your Mobile Phone

The last thing you should do before you start sending tweets is set up your smartphone.

Twitter began with mobiles in mind, so it's not too surprising that although you can have a lot of fun—and a lot of benefits—with Twitter just by using your computer, being able to send and receive tweets from your mobile phone makes the whole experience so much better.

There are a number of different Twitter applications, both from the company itself and from third-party developers, for iPhones, Android phones, and Windows Phone devices.

Once hooked up with your mobile, you can send out an update while waiting for your meal in a restaurant, while you're standing in line at the department of motor vehicles (DMV), or while you're sitting in the audience at a conference listening to a speaker and sharing their ideas with your followers.

Using mobile Twitter applications makes tweeting so much more convenient, and it means that you're much less likely to forget to update.

A Winning Social Media Philosophy

We're just about ready to post your first tweet. But let's pull back from the site for just a few minutes and take a bird's-eye view of social media. What we're about to share with you is pure gold, and understanding and adopting this approach to everything you do online can make all the difference in your results.

Do we have your attention? Get your highlighter ready because you'll use it.

Have you ever been interrupted at your home by a knock on the door from a door-to-door salesperson? Although we have nothing against salespeople, the products or services they offer, or their right to pursue more sales, I think we can all identify with the unsolicited vacuum cleaner salesperson showing up on our doorstep at the most inopportune time.

You may have had a long day at work. Perhaps dinner is on table and the kids are screaming. Or maybe you just want to be left alone. You just know that something is bothering you about opening your door to find a smiling person standing there wanting to sell you something.

Tear away the layers of negative emotions that might surface from such an interaction, and you are left with basic human psychology.

Odds are, the person at your door is not going to have any luck collecting money from you at that time. And it's because you don't trust him or her. Why not? Most likely because you don't know the person. And you probably aren't in the mood to get to know him or her better because you aren't happy with the fact that someone is showing up at your door to sell you something. In other words, you don't like the salesperson.

In other words, you have no existing relationship with this individual that has earned him or her the right to show up on your doorstep and seek to complete a business transaction with you.

And there it is: relationship.

Social media is all about relationship. Life is all about relationship. Whether online or off-line, the business that we do is ultimately not about the product or service we offer but the people whose lives are affected by what we offer. Joel and Dave are not in the business of writing books. We are in the business of enriching people's lives with information they will find valuable and useful.

People buy from those whom they like, know, and trust. It is unlikely that you will fork over your hard-earned cash to someone who hasn't instilled a sense of like, know, and trust in your mind and heart.

The four steps to selling more of anything in the online or off-line world, whether it be a product, service, or idea, are these:

1. Like me.

2. Know me.

3. Trust me.

4. Pay me.

Our friend the vacuum cleaner salesperson often fails at accomplishing goals because he or she hasn't taken the time to build relationship, thereby not allowing the building blocks of like, know, and trust to be put in place first. He or she has jumped directly to number 4, *pay me,* and has attempted to circumvent the natural order of building relationships. It just doesn't work that way.

It's not a difficult concept to grasp, but how many times have you seen someone set up a social media account and immediately begin blasting out his or her company's offers? More times than we can count, we've observed brands jumping right to *pay me* without first building like, know, and trust.

You may have even done this yourself.

Ouch. It's all right. You aren't alone. And the good news is that armed with a better understanding of how relationships are best built, you can start today with a healthier and more effective approach to social media.

So let's apply this philosophy to social media, and Twitter in particular.

When we like someone on Twitter, our first act is to follow him or her.

Doing so allows us to see the tweets that this person is sharing with us. We can easily determine whether the content being shared is commercial in nature or is designed to engage sincerely and honestly with us, the follower.

The content being tweeted helps us *know* the person better. Is he or she bringing value to our Twitter stream and to our lives? Does he or she share valuable content, or is he or she stingy with original thoughts? Does he or she engage with us as human beings or treat us as if we are a collective? When we tweet the person, does he or she reply to us personally or ignore us? As we experience, we decide whether we can *trust* him or her.

If the answer is no, we may choose to unfollow that account. Even worse, we may tell others that the person seems just to want to sell us stuff.

But if the answer is yes, with like, know, and trust being successfully developed, it is but a short hop to pay. In fact, if companies and brands focus on bringing value to their followers by authentically seeking to build relationships with them, the likelihood of a financial transaction taking place increases dramatically.

There's one word in that last paragraph that we believe sums up the whole of success in social media, and in life.

Authenticity.

The aforementioned like, know, and trust are born out of real relationships with real people. Being real means that we recognize our humanity. It means we aren't afraid to be who we are, even as employees of a company. After all, a company is just made up of people.

And we are all people with hopes, dreams, fears, talents, personality, experiences, flaws, and the full range of human emotions that we all share.

This is why people who try to cover up their mistakes tend to get looked down upon. They aren't being real.

There's nothing wrong with making mistakes. We try to make at least one solid mistake each day. That's how we learn!

But owning up to your mistakes is a different story. People, and brands, who are authentic in the way they live out their lives (both publicly and privately) are those most likely to triumph.

The social space is no different. Don't be afraid to be who you are. People are far more accepting of flawed people who own their flaws than those who appear always to have it all together. It's likely because we suspect they are hiding something.

Spending time behind a computer screen and a Twitter account makes it all the easier to hide and pretend to be something you're not. We recommend that you don't succumb to that temptation. Be the best authentic you that you can be, and let people like, know, and trust you for all the right reasons.

We will share a number of strategies and tactics for social media success in the pages to come, but if you've got a hold of this, you have a major leg up on your competition.

And with that said, let's zoom back in and get you started with your first tweet!

Sending Your Very First Tweet

Hit the *Home* link at the top of the page to return to your Twitter page.

There, at the top left of the screen, is Twitter's constant invitation to "Compose new Tweet . . ."

Beneath it is the space for you to write—in 140 characters—an answer.

So off you go.

Type whatever is going through your mind and hit *Tweet*. (See Figure 3.17.)

Figure 3.17   Love your tweet or hate it, once it's up, Twitter gives you options.

Don't worry if you can't think of anything very smart and witty to write. At this stage, you just want to try writing something so that you can see what happens. "Joining Twitter!" is good enough.

Now anyone will be able to read that tweet.

If that sounds like a terrible idea, click the tweet and you'll get a time stamp. Click that time stamp, and you'll get the tweet itself. On the right of the update will be two icons: a star and a trash can.

The star saves the tweet so that you can easily find it again, and the trash can deletes the tweet. There's a good chance that you'll find both of those useful.

Becoming a Follower

And the last thing you need to do before you're ready to start building up your Twitter presence is to follow people.

This is the easiest part of Twitter and really the most enjoyable. So many amazing people are on the site that you shouldn't have any trouble at all finding people whose tweets you want to read and whom you want to follow.

If you already know whom you want to follow on Twitter, just surf to his or her Twitter page and hit the *Follow* button. If not, there's a stack of people in the directory at the back of this book who post very interesting updates.

You're welcome to go to @JoelComm and @DaveTaylor to follow us, too!

A Word about Security

You're almost ready to start building your followers. Before you head out into the Twitterverse, though, a word about security. Twitter's incredible growth has attracted the attention of all sorts of bad guys. There have been incidents of accounts being hacked and taken over, phishing scams, and password theft. President Obama's account was hijacked by a hacker, as was Rick Warren's. Occasionally, you'll see messages flying around Twitter warning you against clicking a link or following a particular person.

In general, it's a good idea to follow those warnings.

It used to be that many apps asked you to enter your Twitter username and password. Bad news. Modern apps use a low-level authorization system called OAuth, so if a site or app is asking for your Twitter password, run away! Much more of an issue, especially for well-known Twitterers, are fake accounts. Anyone can set up a new account and start Twittering in someone else's name. Sometimes the account is clearly fictional, done with honest intentions, and often very well, too. For example, @darthvader is a hilarious satire of the evil *Star Wars* character.

The Don Draper account (@don_draper), which tweets on behalf of the protagonist from the popular American Movie Classics (AMC) TV drama *Mad Men*, was originally created by Paul Isakson (@paulisakson), director of strategy and insights at digital relationships company Space 150. He wanted to find out what would happen if people could actually engage with a TV character and then hand control of the timeline over to the company. AMC wasn't happy and shut him down, but now—smartly—it uses the account to market the show.

Those uses are fine, and as long as the owner of the rights to the name doesn't complain—and when the Twitterer is helping promote the brand, why should he or she?—then Twitter will turn a blind eye.

Much more worrying is when someone tweets deceptively in the name of an individual or a business, using that person's or that brand's trust to sell his or her own goods.

This is a problem that Joel's been battling for some time.

Joel has one account. You can find him on @JoelComm and nowhere else on Twitter. And yet, he's had to report dozens of fake accounts Twittering as @joel_lcomm, @joel_m_comm, and all sorts of other odd combinations that are designed to defraud followers by suggesting that he recommends products that he's never even heard of.

Of course, it's not just Joel. This is a danger for celebrities, and it's a danger for companies. If someone starts Twittering in the name of your business, he or she is stealing your customers—and worse, he or she is stealing your reputation.

Twitter is pretty good about this. Report someone for identify theft on the site by sending the username to @spam, and it will shut the account down fast. But there's nothing stopping him or her from starting up again with a slightly different username.

That's why Twitter has also introduced *verified accounts.* You can see them on the accounts of very well-known Twitterers, such as Ashton Kutcher (@aplusk) and Oprah Winfrey (@Oprah). At the top right of the timeline, you'll be able to see a check mark in a blue cloud background and the phrase *Verified Account.*

So those are the basics. You now know how to set up your Twitter account and create an attractive profile that acts as a marketing tool. And you know how to send tweets and follow people.

Now you can start building up your own followers.

4

Twitter Setup and Design

Twitter Name

WHAT'S IN A NAME?

So, you're about to create your Twitter profile, and you have to think of a name—not your name—but your Twitter username. You will be asked to put in two items: your *real name* and your *username*. The goal is to be purposeful in choosing how you're going to show up on Twitter. Figure 4.1 shows the differences between your real name and username.

> Caution: changing your name or username too much is not a wise action for brand consistency. Be purposeful. Be consistent.

DECISIONS: CHANGE PROFILE OR CREATE NEW PROFILE?

Sometimes during the rebranding phase of your organization, you might want to keep your *old* username as well. The goal would be to communicate through your avatar, bio, and tweets your *new* Twitter account.

This chapter is from contributor Matt Clark of TweetPages—a design company focusing on helping clients brand well in social media. Matt brings more than 15 years of design experience coupled with a passion for making sure you or your organization is branded consistently.

	REAL NAME	USERNAME
WHAT DOES IT DO?	IDENTIFIES **YOU** TO YOUR FRIENDS, COLLEAGUES OR CLIENTS. (MOST LIKELY YOUR PERSONAL NAME)	IDENTIFIES YOUR **ENTITY** TO THE WORLD. THIS COULD BE YOU — PERSONALLY — AS A CELEBRITY, AUTHOR, CONSULTANT, ETC. OR YOUR BUSINESS, NON-PROFIT, CAUSE, ETC.
WHERE DOES IT SHOW UP?	YOUR REAL NAME SHOWS UP ON YOUR PROFILE PAGE	YOUR USERNAME SHOWS UP IN THE VANITY URL, @REPLIES AND DIRECT MESSAGES
CHARACTERS ALLOWED	20 CHARACTERS	15 CHARACTERS
POINTS TO PONDER	IF YOU'RE A **PERSONAL BRAND** YOU'LL WANT TO USE YOUR PERSONAL NAME. (E.G. @JOELCOMM, @DAVETAYLOR, @MICHAELHYATT, @MARISMITH) IF YOU'RE A **BUSINESS/CAUSE/NON-PROFIT** YOU MAY USE THE BUSINESS NAME HERE AS WELL (E.G., @TWEETPAGES, @SONY, @NORTHLANDCHURCH, @ALSASSOCIATION)	TRY TO USE THE SAME USERNAME ACROSS ALL OF YOUR SOCIAL NETWORKS. THIS HELPS WITH BRAND CONSISTENCY. (TWITTER IS THE EASIEST TO CHANGE — BUT LIMITS THE CHARACTERS ALLOWED)
CAN I CHANGE ANYTIME?	**YES** AS AN ENTREPRENEUR I MADE THE CHOICE TO UTILIZE BOTH BIZ NAME AND MY REAL NAME — FOR BRAND RECOGNIZTION WITH A TOUCH OF PERSONAL CONNECTION. E.G., - TWEETPAGES (MATT)	**YES** CHANGING YOUR USERNAME WILL NOT AFFECT @REPLIES, DIRECT MESSAGES OR YOUR EXISTING FOLLOWERS. YOU MAY WANT TO CONSIDER TWEETING YOUR FOLLOWERS (BEFORE YOU CHANGE) THAT YOUR USERNAME WILL CHANGE — BUT THAT YOU STILL PROVIDE THE SAME GREAT PRODUCT/SERVICE AS ALWAYS.

Figure 4.1   The Differences: Real Name versus Username

Look at what they did for Jimmy Fallon when he moved from *Late Night with Jimmy Fallon* to *The Tonight Show Starring Jimmy Fallon.*

He went from @LateNightJimmy to @FallonTonight (see Figure 4.2):

+ The *avatar* (profile picture) says, "We've moved! Follow us: @FallonTonight"

+ The *bio* says, "New show, new Twitter account! We've moved to @FallonTonight" with a link to the *new* Twitter profile.

Figure 4.2   Don't give up the old Twitter handle; just have it point to your new one.

Twitter Setup

THE TWITTER BIO

The Twitter bio is important because it is what people see on the profile page (desktop) and the header (mobile) when perusing Twitter. These 160 characters tell everyone what you're about and what you provide.

I typically use the formula below to create the best award-winning bio possible:

$$X + (2b \times purpose) + jargon = bio$$

Okay—I'm just kidding. There is no formula! But there is a principle: be purposeful. Find your goal. Ask, What do you want people to know? This is tough, because you have to reach deep down to find the right words that explain what you do in 160 characters. This can be daunting—but it doesn't have to be. Below are some tips to consider when creating your bio.

Less is more—Simple and to the point.

Brainstorm—Throw the ideas, sentences, words, and pictures onto a piece of paper.

Read it out loud—Then have someone else read it out loud. Listen to what they emphasize.

Feedback galore—Let your family, friends, coworkers, and clients (and an occasional enemy) read your bio. Get their feedback.

Figure 4.3 Brand identity can be about story, about helping search engines, or about something entirely different.

Your bio section in the Twitter interface gets picked up by search engines whereas the words in your graphics do *not*. I have found many people's and companies' websites by Googling some words, which led me to their Twitter profile, and from there I clicked on their website link.

I always say put the *business keywords* in your bio and the *personality* or *additional info* in your graphics. What are people going to search for you or your business by? This is *not* a hard-and-fast rule, just something to consider. You can still make your bio full of fun—to grab attention—but consider those keywords that you think people might search for to find what you offer. See if you can marry both search engine optimization (SEO) and story. Be real, and be relational.

Overall, consider your purpose.

◆ Your bio should say what they *need* to know to understand what you do or who you are.

◆ Your *graphic* should communicate your *identity*.

How you word it depends on the industry you're in. A consultant would be a little different flavor than a comedian would. And a Fortune 500 company would be different from an entrepreneur (see Figure 4.3).

When putting together content for your social media, website, and so on, we tend to move to one direction or the other: SEO or story. SEO tells us to use every keyword, back link, and tagline to its optimal potential so that when others search—they find you.

The other camp believes that the poetic heartstrings of your story should lead people to find you. (You could say that *story* could also be referred to as *content marketing*). We all would agree that a good narrative moves us all.

In my opinion? You need both SEO and story. It's about balance, using good keywords as you refine your story. And I don't mean *story* as in weaving a tale to get out of your homework. I mean *story* as in communicating the truths that have taken place that have brought you to the position you are in now.

I like how author and freelance copywriter Barry Feldman phrased it— *content optimization*—which hails a pass to making it a both/and scenario. It sure beats my phrase—STEORY.

Here's an example of TweetPages' bio (Figure 4.4):
This does five things:

1. It tells them what we do = *Social Media Branding*

2. It tells them how long we've been around = *2008*

Figure 4.4   Tell the story of your brand in a sentence.

3. It tells them the designs we create (emphasizing custom) = *Twitter, Facebook, YouTube, Google*

4. It tells them where we have been featured (or where they might have seen us) = *Twitter Power & Platform*

5. It gives a call to action to visit our website = *EXPLORE:* tweetpages.com

TweetPages' Graphic

Our TweetPages graphic sometimes includes additional text—but it typically isn't something people would search for (to find us). The graphic gives us the *full* opportunity to continue our branding with consistent colors, patterns, graphics, and more. Of course, this also gives us the opportunity to place the books that we are featured in, in the header.

The Twitter Profile Photo

The profile photo is also referred to as the *avatar*. This is the representation of any social media account. The recommendation is to use the same avatar across all of your social networks for brand consistency. That way others will recognize you when they land on your other networks *or* even your website.

Choosing Your Avatar

The first thing you need to determine is whether you're going to use your logo, your personal photo, or a combination of both. You can determine this by placing yourself in one of three categories of how you're using Twitter:

♦ If you're a medium or large company with multiple employees, *you'll want to use your logo.*

♦ If you're a small business or entrepreneur, *you might consider using your photo* and *logo.*

♦ If you're a solopreneur, personality, and so on, then *you'll want to use your photo.*

Any time you can incorporate your photo somewhere, the better. In the vast expanse of social media networks, people tend to gravitate toward someone with a personal photo over a logo.

Figure 4.5 is a table that can help determine the area you fall in.

TAKING YOUR PHOTO

Not every photo is the same. Run through your list of friends on Twitter, and you'll see that they are not all created equal. Although you don't necessarily have to go out and spend tons of money to get professional head shots, it is generally a good idea (if you have the

	WHAT THIS MEANS	TYPES OF PROFILES	EXAMPLES
LOGO	☑ THIS IS YOUR LOGO ONLY. ☑ ONE FACE CANNOT REPRESENT THE COMPANY. ☑ A WELL-ESTABLISHED BRAND WHERE THE LOGO IS HIGHLY RECOGNIZABLE.	• FORTUNE 500 COMPANIES • CHURCHES • CAUSES/MOVEMENTS • RESTAURANTS* • ETC.	@SONY @SAMSCLUB
PHOTO & LOGO	☑ THIS IS YOUR PHOTO WITH YOUR LOGO COLORS, LOGO MARK OR PATTERNS, INVOLVED IN THE AVATAR.	• ENTREPRENEURS • SMALL BUSINESSES • CONSULTANTS/COACHES • REAL ESTATE AGENTS* • RESTAURANTS* • ETC.	@TWEETPAGES @IMAGEDESIGNS
PHOTO	☑ THIS IS STRICTLY YOUR PHOTO AND NOTHING ELSE. ☑ A RESULT OF YOUR FACE BEING YOUR BRAND MORE THAN A MARK/ICON. ☑ SOMETIMES THIS IS A RESULT OF NOT HAVING A LOGO/BRAND.	• ATHLETES • ARTISTS • AUTHORS • COMEDIANS • MUSICIANS • BLOGGERS • CELEBRITIES • REAL ESTATE AGENTS* • ETC.	@BRIANREGANCOMIC @MICHAELHYATT

Figure 4.5 Logo, photo + logo, or just photo. Here are the trade-offs.

*Multiple types: These are examples where it could go either way. For example, most restaurants would have their logo represented on the avatar. But in some cases where it is recognizable—you would have a photo of the dining (food, outside of building, etc.) *and* the name of the restaurant.

Figure 4.6   Your photo speaks volumes about your brand identity, so carefully consider whether a formal pic is best.

ability) to get professional shots done. It makes all the difference to see photography done by a professional rather than an amateur. Even though software, apps, and cameras help us amateur photographers out, it's always best to leave it up to the pros. I can always tell when our clients hand us photos from someone who knows what he or she is doing rather than selfie shots (see Figure 4.6).

> The world of social media is both forgiving and frightfully biting. Know your audience. As a small business that wants to promote the value of family, authenticity, and approachability—I feel that my audience is okay with my selfie shots @TweetPages. They want to see the underdog, little guy, and up-and-coming business doing good in the world. But I also think that you can take some professional photos and lean them toward a casual feel to reach your target audience. It's best to communicate effectively to your photographer about the look and feel you're after.

With all that said, I realize you may not be able to hire a professional photographer at 1 AM as you create your Twitter profile. So here are some tips to get your photos started in the right direction:

1. Smile and make eye contact—It's amazing how many times someone looks grumpy in his or her profile photo. Unless you're a method actor, take the time to engage with the camera and smile with your eyes.

2. Take lots of photos—If you take three to five photos, you're likely to end up with a photo that you wouldn't put on your Christmas card. But take 15 to 30 and you will

Figure 4.7   SEO Naming Tip

likely find several that you'll love. The more photos you take, the better the chances of you getting a shot that will make your mother proud.

3. Lighting—Adequate lighting is very helpful to get the right shot. If you know how to use Photoshop or Lightroom, you can create the effect of better lighting—but you'll never replace a nicely lit photo. Grab your favorite search engine, look up "DIY photography lighting," and you will find photos, blogs, and videos on how to create great lighting for your photo shoot.

4. Name the photo properly—Remember to remove the default photo name (e.g., IMG43879852895.jpg) to something that is search friendly with your real name *or* your business name. That way when people search for your name or business name, the photo will eventually pop up (e.g., TweetPages-Matt-Clark.jpg). Figure 4.7 provides another tip for naming.

Twitter Interface Basics

Here is the lowdown of how to upload your Twitter graphics. Please note that Twitter changes its interface periodically—but the basics typically remain. In case you're time traveling, this is how we did it back in 2014. And before you proceed, keep in mind the basic trade-off between expensive, slow, professional, and the classic quick and dirty approach.

♦ Making changes from the *profile page* (see Figure 4.8):

  ◇ Log in to your account and press the *Edit profile* button. To change your:

    ○ Header or photo: *Change your header photo or Change your profile photo > Save changes*

Figure 4.8 Find the *Edit profile* button, then remember to *Save changes* when you're done.

- Bio > (click in bio area and type) > *Save changes*
- Theme color > (click on color bar that says *Theme color* and choose or put in Hex code) > *Save changes*

Figure 4.9   Here's where all those useful *Settings* are hiding.

◇ Making changes from the *settings page:*

    ○ To change your username (see Figure 4.9): Log in to your account and click on your miniphoto on the right > Settings > Account > (change username) > *Save changes*

    ○ To change your photo, header, or bio (see Figure 4.10): log in to your account and click on your miniphoto on

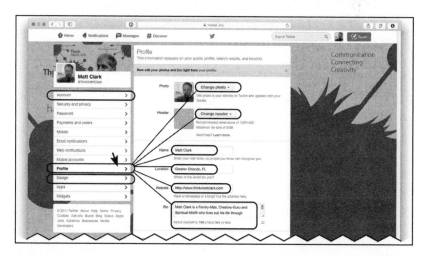

Figure 4.10   Account, Profile, and Design sections are all important to fine-tune for your profile.

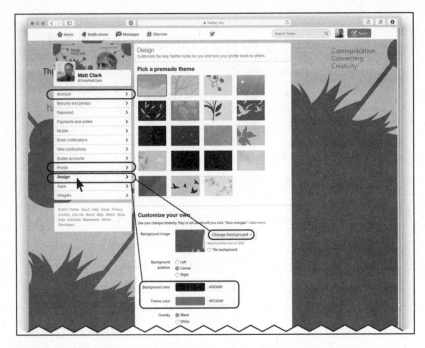

Figure 4.11 Try a few different designs, see how they look!

the right > Settings > Profile > Change photo (upload)
or Change header (upload) *or* (type in bio section) >
Save changes

○ To customize your background color and link color:
log in to your account and click on your miniphoto on
the right > Settings > Design > (add Hex code *or* click
on color bar and mouse to desired color) > *Save
changes*

○ To change your background image (optional; see
Figure 4.11): log in to your account and click on
your miniphoto on right > Settings > Design >
Change background (upload) *or* click *Remove* and
use the *Background color* option (recommended) >
Save changes

Twitter Graphics

TIME, TALENT, AND TOOLS

I always say if you have the time, talent, and tools, then you don't need us. Some have the *talent*, but their *time* is too valuable to spend on designing graphics. Some have the *time*, but they lack the *tools*. And yet others' deficit is the initial *talent* to put a proficient design together.

But the reality is there are many in between, and you have to decide where you fit in. Below you'll find three different ways to get your graphics started. Ask yourself the questions in Figure 4.12.

THE QUICK AND EASY

The quick and easy is all about setting up your graphics the fastest way possible to be up and running in no time. This is the abridged way to get started. After you complete your Twitter sign-up process, you'll want to upload your Twitter avatar (profile

FREE SOFTWARE	PAID SOFTWARE	ONLINE CREATORS
INKSCAPE	ADOBE ILLUSTRATOR OR PHOTOSHOP (MONTHLY SUBSCRIPTIONS START FROM $9.99 UP TO $49.99)	CANVA.COM (FREE AND PAID).
GIMP AND GIMPSHOP		CANVA HAS SO MUCH TO OFFER. FROM SOCIAL MEDIA TO BUSINESS CARDS. FROM FLYERS TO BLOG
SUMOPAINT		GRAPHICS. YOU CAN UPLOAD YOUR OWN GRAPHICS. USE SOME OF THEIRS FOR FREE OR PAY A
SKETCH (FREE IPAD APP)	AFFINITY DESIGNER ($49.99)	MINIMAL FEE FOR ADDITIONAL GRAPHICS, BACKGROUNDS, PHOTOS AND MORE.
PICMONKEY (FREE AND PAID) PHOTO EDITING, COLLAGE AND DESIGN	CORELDRAW (SUITE $499)	AUTREPLANETE SOCIAL NETWORKS ONLY UPLOAD OWN GRAPHICS. AUTREPLANETE.COM/AP-SOCIAL-MEDIA-IMAGE-MAKER/

NOT A COMPREHENSIVE LIST

Figure 4.12 How much you pay for graphics and images is determined by more than just your budget.

picture). Based on the sections above you'll have a better handle on what you want to be seen in your avatar. Once you have your username and avatar, you'll want to make the header the same color as your website.

If you already have a logo designed for you, I would reference the color from your logo. If you have only a website, then use an online tool (eyedropper) to find out some of the colors on your website.

A few tools to do this are:

Mac: Use DigitalColor Meter on your system

Mac or PC: Download and install ColorZilla for Firefox or Chrome

PC: Download Instant Eyedropper

Below are requirements for size dimensions for the current Twitter layout.

♦ The current dimensions for avatars are 400 × 400 pixels.

♦ The current dimensions for header graphics are 1,500 × 500 pixels.

♦ Photos can be in any of the following formats: Joint Photographic Experts Group (JPG), graphic interchange format (GIF), or portable network graphics (PNG).

♦ Twitter does not support animated GIFs for profile or header images.

Head over to www.TweetPages.com/TwitterPowerThreePoint Oh to grab your *free* templates for the avatar and header graphics.

THE DIY OF TWITTER GRAPHICS

This is where it gets fun. This one takes the most time—but for some it is very rewarding when you have accomplished creating your own design. There are many options to do it yourself, and

	QUICK & EASY	D.I.Y.	CUSTOM
WHAT IS MY TIME FRAME?	I WANT IT DONE IMMEDIATELY TO MOVE ON TO OTHER ITEMS.	I WANT TO SPEND THE TIME TWEAKING MY DESIGN CONTENT. (NOTE: YOU MAY NEED TO EXPLORE TO FIND ALL THE SOCIAL NETWORKS.)	I WANT TO MAXIMIZE MY TIME ON SOMETHING ELSE. (I WANT MY DESIGNS TO BE CONSISTENT WITH MY BRAND.)
WHAT IS MY COST?	FREE	FREE AND LOW–COST TOOLS AVAILABLE.	HIGHER COST FOR CUSTOM DESIGN WORK.
WHAT IS MY DESIGN INVOLVEMENT?	LOW	MEDIUM–HIGH	NONE (A PROFESSIONAL DESIGNER HANDLES THE CREATIVE FOR YOU)

Figure 4.13   The DIY of Twitter Graphics

Figure 4.13 shows three ways that you can create your own graphics for Twitter.

Free Software

Free software allows you to download and explore each one on your own time. There are plenty of tips and tutorials out there to help you along. Although each software has its own scope of support—from none to surprisingly good—be assured that you can reach out to your fellow Twitter users for help. Some of these (e.g., PicMonkey) have an online component where you do everything through your web browser.

Paid Software

These have a substantial range of cost—from $50 to $500. There are even monthly plans available starting at $9.99 a month. Adobe is the industry standard for professionals to create content. Most of these types of software are programs that you have to download to your computer. Before you purchase, read the system requirements for each one. Some cater to PC, some to Mac, and some to both.

Online Creators

I have separated these out because they specifically have two things in common: (1) they are online and (2) they distinctly have social media sizes. That way you're not out there guessing the pixel size of a Twitter header (although we've given the current size to you in this chapter). Each of these listed not only has Twitter—but some of the other social networks, too.

Want to find more? Head over to AlternativeTo.net to find alternative software for just about anything.

Tools to Use

I can't tell you how many times I've needed some strange tool and found it online. The content below is of some handy (and random) tools that you can use.

WhatTheFont (MyFonts.com/WhatTheFont/): Have you seen a font and not been sure what it is? This is a great font tool to determine what a particular font is. It's not perfect—but it does find the closest matches in its giant font database. You can even submit the font for other font enthusiasts to take a stab at what they think it is. Basically you can take a screenshot of a word, font, or letter and upload it. It will spill out potential candidates for you to use. Note: This font database is for purchase—and well worth it. Although there are *free* fonts out there—be forewarned—because many fonts are not made correctly and will affect your computer. Good typography is worth the money paid.

Letter and character counter (MyLetterCounter.com): This is a free online tool that counts letters, characters, and words in one fell swoop. You can't go wrong for composing tweets, short message service (SMS) text messages, and articles and crafting word length for SEO purposes.

Some items to count:

◊ Twitter's character limit is 140.

◊ SMS text message limit is 160.

◊ Google AdSense ads can have 25 characters for the title, 70 characters for the ad text, and 35 characters for the displayed uniform resource locator (URL).

Note: counting letters = counting characters (the spaces between words).

Alphabetizer (Alphabetizer.flap.tv): Do you have a list that needs to be alphabetized? This is the handy website that allows you to copy and paste your list to your end product.

The website says: "The Alphabetizer was created as a tool to alphabetize and sort lists online using your computer or mobile device. This web tool and educational resource provides sort functions including the ability to: do abc or alphabetical order, remove HTML [hypertext markup language], capitalize and lowercase words and phrases, ignore case, order names, sort by last name, add numbers, letters and roman numerals to lists, and more. Visitors can use this gadget on their tablets, phones and computers to help with homework or business or just for fun! Oh, and it's free!"

HOW TO BUY CUSTOM TWITTER DESIGNS

There are tons of ways to purchase custom Twitter designs on the Internet. You won't find a shortage of people who are able to take your content to the next level. The key is branding consistently. Make sure designers are able to deliver a high-quality design that fits your overall look and feel of your identity.

Below are some questions to consider before buying:

- ◆ Is the designer experienced?

- ◆ Does the designer understand the ever-changing dynamics of designing for Twitter?

- ◆ Can he or she design for other social networks, too?

- ◆ Does he or she have a portfolio to show you the style of designs he or she creates?

- ◆ What are the final files you receive?

- ◆ Does he or she upload the graphics for you?

- ◆ Does he or she design with mobile, desktop, and multiple resolutions in mind?

Obviously, things such as turnaround, pricing, edits, and future changes all need to be considered.

There is custom work and then there is custom work.

Design is more about listening to the client fully, collaborating creatively, and relieving him or her of any of the work. A competent designer should give you the freedom to move on to the other projects and return to you with great designs. Leave the creative lifting for the custom designer. Unfortunately, some just move things around on a page. Their ability to think about adequate white space, attention to detail, colors, and branding may not be up to par. They may say custom—but many are passing template work off as custom. Look through their portfolio and have a conversation with them. Not all custom work is created equal.

Now . . . What about TweetPages?

Of course, we'd be more than happy to design for you. TweetPages has been around since 2008. We design to the latest specs for social networks. Let us know how we can help: hello@tweetpages.com.

Building a Following on Twitter

Websites have users, Facebook has friends, and Twitter has followers. They follow your messages—and, in the process, they follow your life.

Unlike users or Facebook friends, though, followers don't have to make any effort to enjoy your content. The tweets that you write can come to them, even directly to their smartphone if they want.

Like users and Facebook friends, followers are valuable. The more followers you have, the further your messages will reach and the more influence you'll have. (See Figure 5.1.)

As always on the Internet, it can take time to build a large community of readers—certainly more time than most impatient publishers like to commit. But it's worth the effort, and there are a number of things that you can do to reduce that time and build your list quickly.

The most important is the piece of advice that remains golden whatever you're doing on the Internet: produce content that's interesting, fun, and valuable.

Tweets are supposed to describe what you're doing right now, but they can also include opinions, announcements, and conversations. You can write anything you want. You can even include links in your tweets to send people for further reading. Clearly, *that* can be very useful!

But remember if all you do is tell people about your new product or try to send them to some sales or affiliate site, you'll

Figure 5.1 It's nice to be popular. This is how Joel's followers look to other Twitter users. Browsing follower lists is a good way to find people you want to follow. The button on the right allows you to follow other people directly from the list.

soon find that you have no followers at all, or at least no followers who pay attention to what you're posting, which can be even worse.

Don't forget that some of your followers will be receiving your tweets on their phones. That means that they might be paying for them. If they don't think that they're getting value for their money—whether that's entertainment value, advice value, or any other kind of value—they'll stop following.

You don't have to pay money for Twitter followers, but you do have to pay with good content—written in 140 characters or fewer.

In this chapter, I'm going to explain how to build your followers. As you follow these strategies, though, bear in mind that the best way to create a long list of followers—*and the only way to keep them reading and engaged*—is always to create great content, and on Twitter that means generating interesting conversations that other people want to join.

Quantity or Quality: Choosing the Type of Following You Want

If you want masses and masses of followers, there's really nothing to it. It's a breeze. It's simple. It's almost foolproof.

Simply browse Twitter and follow everyone you see.

Some of those people will follow you in return automatically. Others will follow you out of basic online etiquette (though we don't believe that it's good etiquette to automatically follow anyone who choses to follow you on Twitter, as is obvious by both of our follower ratios, as discussed in Chapter 3).

In one experiment, Stefan Tanase (@stefant), a Romanian security researcher, created a Twitter account with the username Osen Komura (@osen). He found that simply following almost 50,000 people give him nearly 8,000 followers in return, a follow-back rate of about 17 percent.

It's possible. You can do it. And if you're desperate to have a large Twitter following, you could try it.

But we don't recommend it, and neither of us would use this particular strategy, for a number of reasons.

The first is that it's going to take you a huge amount of time. It's going to be very tedious, and it's going to clog your Twitter feed with tons of messages from people you really don't care to follow.

In other words, by following the maximum number of people possible to gain followers yourself, you're agreeing to be spammed in return for doing some spamming yourself. And you're tacitly admitting that you're going to ignore the people you now follow—because there are just too darn many of them. How can you expect they won't be ignoring you in return?

That's going to turn what should be a really fun experience into something that you're not going to do for very long.

The second reason this is a bad tactic is that Twitter will make it hard. If there's a large gap between the number of people you're following and the number who follow you, Twitter will stop you following any more people as a way to prevent spam accounts like those that might follow 25,000 people but have only 10 to 15 followers.

No single number or ratio triggers that block. According to Twitter's Following Rules and Best Practices page, "this limit is different for every user and is based on your ratio of followers to following."

The most important reason for not building your followers by following as many people as you possibly can is that it just doesn't work for marketing your products or services.

Why? Because in that situation at best a small number will actually read your tweets. A small fraction will want to join your conversations. And when you send out a tweet about your new product, your new blog post, or the release of your new e-book, only a tiny number of your followers will pay attention.

That doesn't mean that you shouldn't want a large Twitter following. Obviously, lots of interested followers are always going to be better than a few interested followers. But the price to pay for having a large number of followers is often a less targeted market and a lower conversion rate of followers to customers or users of your own site.

On the other hand, target only those people with a direct interest in your topic, and you'll be able to keep them active and engaged, even if there are fewer of them in total. But, on the other, other hand, if you target too narrowly, you'll be missing other people who might well be interested in what you have to say.

Ah! Decisions, decisions!

What should you do? Should you attempt to build as large a following as possible by following tons of people, or should you try to create as targeted a Twitter community as possible?

Either way, you want a core group of followers who are very interested in your topic, as many people as possible with a mild interest in your topic, and a few people who might be occasionally interested in some aspects of your topic.

Level of interest is not easy to measure, and the chance that you'll turn a vaguely interested follower into a loyal customer depends not only on your engagement with them but also on your product and even market segment. If you're using your

Twitter community to drive people to a website to purchase information products about fantasy football, for example, you might be able to convert a fair number of people who have an interest in sports, even if they don't currently play fantasy football.

If you tweet about lacrosse, though, you'll probably struggle. It's just not as popular a sport, nor are lacrosse fans used to a thriving marketplace of info products, books, biographies, games, posters, calendars, and so on. In that case, a smaller, more focused group of followers would then be much more valuable than a large one.

One factor in deciding whether to go for as large a group as possible or focus on a select group is to assess the broadness of your topic's appeal pragmatically:

- ◆ If your topic is very popular—sports or cars, for example— you could do well with a large group of followers.

- ◆ If your topic appeals only to a small crowd—polo or solar- powered cars—then you might do better narrowing down your follower base and expectations.

The broadness of a topic's appeal isn't the same as the size of its niche either: a marketer who had a website selling Corvette aftermarket parts, for example, would be operating in a small niche, even though the topic itself could be of interest to anyone who likes cars.

When you're considering whom to target for your followers, start with those most interested in your topic, and then expand to add people who might be interested in some of the topics you'll cover in your tweets.

Clearly, there's no scientific formula here.

The balance that you create between a highly targeted group of enthused, engaged Twitter followers and a more general, less involved crowd will often end up based on instinct, a feeling that you have about your chances of bringing in people with only a slight interest in your topic.

That feeling comes from experience and from an understand- ing of your subject and its audience. But it is also important to understand the difference between those two types of followers and try to include both in your follower list.

So, how do you go about finding high-quality followers?

Quality: How to Be Intentional about Creating Your Own Network of Experts

High-quality, engaged followers can do different things. Some will be the type of followers who hang on to your every tweet, follow all your links, take your recommendations quite seriously, and even buy your products.

You certainly want to have lots of those—but identifying them isn't easy.

Few Twitter users write on their bios that they are looking to buy lots of Corvette replacement parts or are obsessed with acquiring every product related to fantasy football—or anything else.

What you can find on Twitter are *experts.*

This is really Twitter's strength. The site is stuffed with people who have deep knowledge and a wealth of information about particular subjects and who are willing to share it.

Find experts on a topic related to yours and encourage them to follow you, and you'll be building yourself a very valuable network.

The first thing you have to do is find them.

Twitter has never had a very good search engine. If you were looking for a particular user on the site, you could toss his or her name into the search engine and hope something came up.

But that was about it.

Looking for keywords or hashtags was also a huge pain, and the results just weren't up to scratch. These days, you can also use Twitter's lists feature, which lets Twitterers categorize their followers by subject. But few people use lists because they're not front and center in the Twitter interface, so they're rarely comprehensive or particularly helpful.

One of the best things about Twitter, though, is that it lets developers create their own tools for the site. As we'll see later in this book, some of those tools can be very valuable. One tool was so valuable that Twitter decided to buy it. Summize's search engine is now a part of Twitter and can be reached by surfing directly to search.twitter.com (see Figure 5.2) or by clicking the search link at the bottom of a Twitter page.

You'll find a bunch of trending topics—a list of the most popular subjects that people are currently discussing—and a search field in which you can enter your keywords and pull up tweets that contain that phrase.

You'll then be able to see who's talking about your topic and, by looking at the bios and reading their tweets, see which of those Twitterers are experts and which are, well, not so much experts.

Search is also now integrated into Twitter itself. On the right side of the page, you'll find a search field and, more important, have the option to save your searches. That makes it very simple to follow the conversations around your most important topics.

If you want to keep track of what people are saying on Twitter about your company or your products, simply search for that keyword and then save the search.

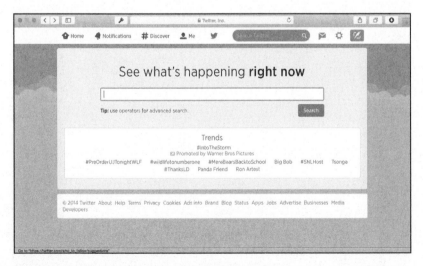

Figure 5.2 To search deeply on Twitter, you have to get off Twitter and hop over to search.twitter.com.

You'll be able to monitor those conversations with just one click!

You can do exactly the same thing when you're looking for experts to follow. There's nothing wrong with searching from your Twitter page instead of from Twitter's search engine. But the search engine is much more powerful. The Advanced Search feature lets you define your search much more powerfully, as shown in Figure 5.3. You can search for complete phrases or tweets by certain people, within a specific area, within a certain time period, with links, and even with smileys.

Whichever search field you use, though, finding the experts in your field is important.

If you wanted to tweet about fantasy football, for example, then all of the people who came back in the search results for that

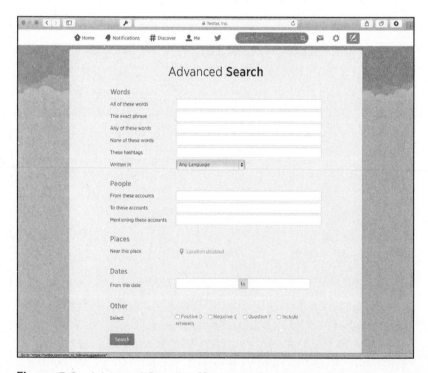

Figure 5.3 Advanced Search offers some impressive options!

phrase would be potential followers. You could try following them all and hope that they follow you back, but that's going to take a while. (See Figure 5.4.)

It's much more efficient to identify the key Twitterers on the topic and get them to follow you.

If other people see that the expert is following you, they'll assume that you're also an expert and want to follow you, too.

Do you see how that works?

One way to succeed on Twitter is to hang out with the thought leaders and influencers. Find the top people in your topic, and become a part of their community.

When you're one of the prominent Twitterers, you'll find it's much easier to persuade people to read and engage with your tweets. In fact, you won't have to do anything but make sure that your tweets are interesting, informative, and entertaining.

Figure 5.4   Search for the phrase "fantasy football" on Twitter, and you get a huge list of responses. Clue for finding experts: experts usually put pictures on their profiles. Also notice it's a real-time search and that there have already been 40 new tweets since the search results were delivered.

And the best news is that getting in with the expert crowd on Twitter is much easier than becoming part of the in crowd at high school.

There are three simple steps.

IDENTIFY THE EXPERTS

Once you've built your list of people who have mentioned your topic in their tweets, you'll need to narrow it down to find the key influencers.

Good signs to look out for in the search results include a picture in the profile and frequent posts, along with their followers:following ratio.

Experts understand the value of all of those factors.

You can also try tweaking your search to include terms such as *guide, guru, expert,* or *author* to help identify leaders.

> Truth be told, however, we'd also counsel that you remain at least a bit skeptical of people who describe themselves as gurus, because that might just be a bit overly self-aggrandizing, suggesting that they actually aren't the gurus that they'd like to be. Read their tweets and ascertain for yourself before you decide to follow them and join their community.

When you find people who look like they might be candidates for your experts list, check to see how many followers they have and when they last updated. There's no minimal number of followers a Twitterer must have to become an expert—too much depends on the topic—*but there is one sign that marks out the experts on Twitter, and it's crucial to your understanding of the site.*

Twitter is the Internet's watercooler. But hang out at your company's watercooler, and you'll find that some people are more influential than others. They're the ones who set the topics, build groups around them, and direct the conversation. It's a dynamic that happens whenever people get together. Whether it's based on charisma, knowledge, confidence, energy, enthusiasm, motivation, or who knows what else, it doesn't matter. At every party and every gathering, communities form around particular individuals.

That happens on Twitter, too. And on Twitter you can spot the individuals around whom those communities form by comparing the number of people they follow with the number of people who follow them. (See Figure 5.5.)

Most of the tweets come from a small minority of Twitterers. That's no different from a party where most of the talking is done by a small number of people—the people with the best stories, the most outgoing personalities, and the easiest way with small talk.

Those are exactly the people you want to find in your topic area. They're the hub around which your community operates, and they're the group of thought leaders you want to join.

Figure 5.5 Andru Edwards is a tech expert who frequently appears on TV, and his commentary and reviews have made him a must follow for gearheads. That expertise is reflected in the ratio between the number of people Edwards is following and the number of his followers. At almost 1:12, it's clear that people are following Edwards to read what he has to say about his topic.

Whatever your topic, it shouldn't take you too long to produce a list of at least a dozen people who are experts to some degree in your field.

Read their tweets and follow them.

GAIN THEIR FRIENDSHIP AND RESPECT

So far, all you've done is identify an expert and followed his or her updates.

This tactic is going to make your Twitter stream considerably more interesting, but it's not going to turn that expert into your follower automatically. It's going to turn you into his or her follower.

To be seen as an expert, you need to stand out both in the community of people he or she is following on Twitter and on his or her personal timeline.

This level of visibility happens only when you turn that Twitter connection into a friendship and a relationship started with shared interests but ultimately cemented by mutual respect.

Twitter provides a couple of tools to do that.

You can hit the reply icon next to one of his or her tweets, or you can send him or her a direct message.

In general, replies are better for a number of reasons. One big one: all of your followers will be able to see your interaction with the expert. Even if the expert doesn't respond, other people will see that you're following him or her and that you have something to contribute to the debate.

That already starts to make you look like an expert, too.

And if the expert responds, then you've hit the jackpot. All his or her followers will see that tweet and can stop by to learn more about you and hopefully follow you. You can start to pick up a lot of valuable followers that way, especially if you continue the conversation with those new followers.

Direct messages are useful only if you have a special request, and you should use them only once you've already attracted the expert's attention through your tweets and your replies, and ideally after letting that expert know that you're sending him or her a direct message.

Otherwise, it's too much like sending a cold e-mail to someone and hoping he or she responds. If the person doesn't, if he or she sees your message as spam, it's also unlikely that he or she will respond to a reply, so you'll have lost the opportunity to start a conversation in public, too. And that's if he or she *sees* the direct message. With so much direct message spam, most popular Twitter users have long since learned to ignore their direct messages inbox.

However you plan to make yourself noticed, do be careful. No one is going to appreciate being bothered by everyone who follows him or her. Twitter might be a very friendly, open place where it's remarkably easy to exchange messages with the kind of people you'd really struggle to meet anywhere else, but if you want to build a friendship, you still have to pay your dues.

The key? Always add value. Always give back more than you take. Here's what we mean . . .

GIVE BACK MORE THAN YOU TAKE

To successfully use the tactic of following experts and getting them to engage with you, you'll have to give the expert, and by extension his or her online community, information that's truly valuable.

Tell experts something they don't already know.

Point them in the direction of a resource they might find helpful.

You can even try tweeting a link if it really will make a difference to the discussion. (Links are a dime a dozen so if you're going to reply with a link as a way of attracting attention, the content has to be really good.)

And you need to hand over this valuable information as often as you can.

Twitter works because people are prepared to share valuable knowledge for free. Some of that knowledge might look worthless, but let's be candid: if it really is worthless, that Twitterer will quickly become shunned and ignored by his or her online community.

When you show people that you have valuable knowledge to share, you'll stand out—even to other experts.

Building up a collection of experts as part of your own community will take time. Some of that time will be spent searching. Some of it will be spent reading tweets—that can be very addictive. Some of it will be spent updating your own Twitter stream so that you come across as an active member of the community.

And some of it will be spent replying to other experts in your field.

As you're doing all of this, you should find that your number of followers starts to grow—both with people you know and respect and with the people who follow and respect them.

Quantity: Seven Killer Strategies to Reaching Critical Mass on Twitter

There are two kinds of follower lists. There are targeted follower lists made of a few people with a strong interest in your topic, and there are general follower lists made up of lots of people with a weaker interest in your topic.

Although you'll want your list to have a mixture of both types of followers, the balance between them will depend on the nature of your topic.

We've seen that adding targeted people can be difficult. It's enjoyable and interesting, and you'll learn a great deal reading the tweets of experts in your field, but it will take time and does depend on good tweet content and good replies.

Creating a large, general follower list can be a lot easier.

But beyond creating great content, you need to keep a couple of important principles. Let's go through them, one by one.

> You have to participate to engage—you have to become an active follower.

You can follow all sorts of people on Twitter. You can follow people you know, people you don't know, and people you'd like to know.

Each time you become someone's follower, you turn up in his or her list, which means that the person can see that you're following him or her and so can everyone else.

You don't have to ask the person's permission—all tweets are public unless the Twitterer restricts them—and you don't have to wait for him or her to approve you. All you have to do is hit the *Follow* button, and that person's tweets become part of your Twitter stream.

Once you've found someone to follow on Twitter, you can see whom they're following and who's following them. If any of those people look interesting, you can add them to your follow list—and continue.

That could be all you need to do to win followers, but that would be slow going and inefficient.

> The other principle you need to use is to join the conversation.

So far, we've been describing Twitter as though the information flow were only one way. That isn't the case at all. Although the main use of Twitter is to let other people know what you're doing, thinking, or listening to at any moment in time, the service also acts like a public slow-motion instant messenger.

You can ask questions and provide answers to the questions other people ask.

In fact, the ability to get great answers on Twitter is one of its biggest strengths. The entire site acts like a giant forum in which experts on all sorts of subjects are willing to lend their advice to almost anyone who asks for it.

It's something that makes Twitter a very valuable resource. Every time you respond, you contribute to someone else's conversation. That makes you a valuable part of the community, and it increases the chances that other people will follow you, too.

Building a long list of followers doesn't happen overnight. It comes as a result of networking on the site, providing good tweets that other people want to read, and being active in other people's discussions.

It's the reward that comes from participating on Twitter, and best of all, it's a lot of fun to do.

But it is important. Twitter really took off once it achieved a critical mass of users—when enough people were using it that the tweets were interesting to read and there was a good chance that you could find someone you wanted to follow.

Critical mass is important to your follower list, too.

You need to have enough followers to enable your tweets to spark a conversation.

You need to have enough followers to be able to convert at least some of them to customers, users, or clients.

And you need to have enough followers to spread word of your tweets and inspire other Twitterers to tell their friends about you.

Although there aren't any foolproof shortcuts to creating your list, there are a few things that you can do to cut the time and build your list faster.

Here are seven different ways to do it.

Look for People You Already Know

Let's start with the very easiest method.

Look for people you already know.

Twitter is popular enough now for there to be a good chance that at least some of the people in your address book are already Twittering away.

As we've seen, Twitter lets you find those people on the site by scanning through your AOL, Gmail, Yahoo!, or Outlook address book. Initially, we recommended that you *not* do this because it's a better idea to wait until your profile has been created and you've started posting tweets.

Once you've done that, though, you're free to let Twitter compare its registered user list against your own contacts.

Just hit the *Find friends* link at the bottom of the *who to follow* box on your Twitter page (not the page with your feed, the page that's about you), or use https://twitter.com/who_to_follow /import to get there faster. (See Figure 5.6).

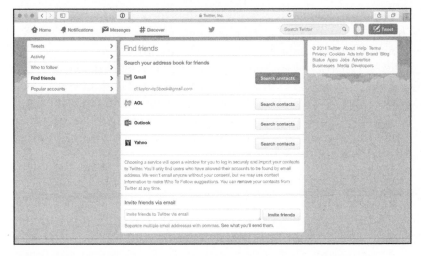

Figure 5.6   Find friends on Twitter the easy way: through your address book.

Choose the service you work with and click on *Search contacts.* The service you've chosen will confirm that you want to grant Twitter permission to analyze your address book, and then Twitter will return a list of all the people who are also using Twitter. Follow them, reply to some of their tweets, or send them a personal message to make sure that they see you're following them, and there's a good chance they'll follow you, too.

That's the good news.

The bad news is that this works only for Web-based mail.

At the moment, there is no simple way to search your PC- or Mac-based address book for Twitterers.

So you'll have to cheat.

Open a free Web-based e-mail account, such as Gmail or Yahoo! Mail, if you don't have one already; then export your contact list from Outlook, Apple Mail, or whatever other e-mail program you prefer; and then import the data into your new account. Your new mail service will explain how to do it, and it shouldn't take more than a few minutes.

You won't have to actually use that account, but you will now be able to search through those contacts automatically on Twitter to see if any of them are also Twitter users.

How many followers will this method give you?

It depends on the size of your contact list and whether your community tends to be Twitter fans. You're unlikely to pick up thousands of followers right away, but there is a good chance that you'll be able to add a few new readers, and there's an excellent chance that those people will follow you in return.

Tweet Your Blog

One of the most common goals of a good Twitter presence will be to direct followers to a website. But this can go both ways, too: you can include your Twitter stream on your blog or website, too. (See Figure 5.7.)

When Ken Denmead tweets a link to his blog, people check it out. Smart. Once they reach his site, his Twitter followers will be able to read his posts that are quite a bit longer than 140 characters. They'll be able to click on his ads, and they'll be able to buy his products.

Figure 5.7   Ken Denmead adds his tweet stream to his popular Geekdad blog at www.geekdad.com.

They won't be able to take any of those particular actions on his Twitter page.

So another one of your goals is to build a closer connection with the users you have so that you become a part of their lives. That means your users will return to your site more often, and they'll be more likely to take you up on your special offers.

Those users then are a valuable pool of potential followers.

If you can show your users your tweets and bring them to your Twitter page, you'll be able to increase the number and engagement level of your followers massively.

And Twitter makes it very easy to post tweets on a website.

If you want to add your tweets to a blog or another Web page you manage, go to Settings > Widgets and choose *Create New*. Or use the shortcut https://twitter.com/settings/widgets/new and start tweaking and tuning the results. (See Figure 5.8.)

Once you've finished customizing it, click on *Create widget* and copy the code. Insert the single line of hypertext markup language (HTML) where you want the tweets to appear on your

Figure 5.8 Twitter's own widgets make publicizing your tweets as simple as click, cut, and paste.

page or site template, and then upload and check to see the widget is looking the way it should.

As always, it's a good idea to make the customization match the design of your site as closely as possible. You want your tweets to look like they're part of your site so that readers see them as extra content, not something that's been brought in from outside—such as an ad.

The result should be that you'll have extra content on your site, your users will be able to see your tweets on your Web page, and they'll be able to click through easily to your Twitter page to see all the tweets they missed. And follow you!

If you're getting thousands of users to your website every week, and only a small percentage of them go through the steps needed to follow you on Twitter, you can still end up with a decent number of followers over time using this strategy.

Twitter also allows you to place a module showing tweets about a particular topic. Twitter calls these Search Widgets, and although they can add some valuable free content to a website, they won't increase your followers on Twitter. They might, though, increase someone else's following on Twitter.

For WordPress users, the news doesn't look quite the same. In fact, it's even better.

If you're running WordPress, a far better option is to use one of the many Twitter plug-ins. Start at wordpress.org/plugins and you'll find more than 1,000 different options. Yikes!

Fortunately, the Jetpack suite of plug-ins from the WordPress development group includes both a widget that lets you include Tweets on your blog pages and another plug-in that lets you automatically issue tweets every time you post a new entry. Check Jetpack.me for more info.

Of course, you can also just ask your website users to follow you on Twitter.

Or rather, you can *tell* them to follow you on Twitter, because according to interface design expert Dustin Curtis (@dcurtis), the way websites tell users to follow them on Twitter has a dramatic effect on the click-through rate.

Saying simply "I'm on Twitter" produces a click-through rate of 4.7 percent—a respectable figure. Ordering users to "Follow me on twitter," however, increases that click-through rate by 55 percent, pushing it up to 7.31 percent. Making the phrase more personal by saying, "You should follow me on twitter" increased the click-through rate to 10.09 percent, and providing a link for people to click in the phrase "You should follow me on twitter here" was the most effective of all, with a click-through rate of 12.81 percent.

Interestingly, the last three figures were true only when Dustin wrote the name of the site without a capital letter—*twitter* rather than *Twitter*. Capitalizing the name of the site reduced the click-through rate by as much as 6 percent.

So, if you want almost one in eight of your site's users to follow you on Twitter, you need to tell them where to go and what to do.

But then again, that's really marketing and ad copy 101, isn't it? All good marketers already know that telling their audience what to do significantly improves results.

Pay Your Followers!

This might not sound like the smartest—or the cheapest—way to bring in large numbers of followers, but you could just consider paying people to follow you.

Giving away freebies is a marketing standard. You create goodwill, let potential customers try your products before they buy, and build a list of clients that you can draw on in the future.

As long as you follow the simple rule that what you give away should cost you little but have high value to the recipient, you should find that offering freebies can have a fantastic effect on your revenues.

Joel's given away hundreds of thousands of dollars' worth of goods through his websites and seminars, and he's definitely received many times that in return.

The principle can work in exactly the same way on Twitter to incentivize Twitterers to follow you.

Mike Wells (@MikeWellsAuthor) is a best-selling thriller and suspense author who uses Twitter to gain followers and readers. As he states in his bio, follow him, and you'll get a free e-book. (See Figure 5.9.)

Figure 5.9   Mike Wells promises in his bio that followers will get a free e-book from the best-selling author.

Now let's be honest. E-mailing that book would have cost him nothing. In fact, when he follows up by sending his followers a link to the e-book, he's also establishing a one-to-one relationship with them through Twitter.

Giving away that book actually paid him by giving him something more valuable in return: a targeted list of followers who are also fans.

It also gave his followers a taste of his writing that will hopefully turn them into customers who seek out and buy his other books and related works.

The *Palo Alto Weekly* (@paloaltoweekly), based in Silicon Valley, takes a slightly different approach. Rather than rewarding Twitterers immediately when they follow its account, the *Palo Alto Weekly* offers rewards in the form of time-limited discount codes in its tweets. (See Figure 5.10.)

For anyone interested in keeping up with the news in Palo Alto, following the company's tweets pays. And the company gets to make sure that people read its news, people are aware of

Figure 5.10 The *Palo Alto Weekly* pays its followers to keep in touch by offering Twitter-only coupons and promotions—and generates sales, too.

campaigns from its advertisers, and it gains even more visibility each time a promotional campaign is launched.

RESPOND TO REQUESTS

One topic that we're going to keep coming back to in this book is that successful Twitterers use Twitter to do more than make announcements.

They use it to spark conversations. And they use it to *join* conversations.

Those conversations are open and public, but that just means that they're even more valuable. When anyone can see who's saying what in a Twitter exchange, anyone can follow the links back to the Twitterers who impress them and follow them as well.

Sometimes that might just mean hitting the *reply* button and coming up with a good response. Often though, other Twitterers offer golden opportunities to jump into a chat by asking a question.

Provide a good answer, and you get to look like a bigger expert than the original Twitterer.

There are a couple of rules to follow here, though.

The first is that any information you provide has to be genuinely good. Saying, "Yeah, I'm having trouble with that, too . . ." or quoting from Wikipedia is not going to do you much good.

People will follow your tweets only if they feel that you have information that's worth reading. That's one reason it's a good idea to answer questions about your subject rather than any question you happen to see.

You'll pick up people with an interest in your topic, but you'll also get a bigger opportunity to show off your expertise.

The second rule is that the more popular the questioner, the greater the benefits of lending him or her a hand—or even providing him or her a good reply. (See Figure 5.11.)

When a superpopular Twitter personality thanks you or comments back, lots of people will see the response, wonder who you are, and stop by your Twitter page to find out.

Figure 5.11 John Cleese (@JohnCleese) is a popular British comedian with more than 3 million followers who retweets, replies to fans, and engages in conversation. Interact, and perhaps he'll respond to you!

MOBILIZE YOUR SOCIAL NETWORK

Twitter is extremely powerful, but it becomes even more powerful when it's used as one part of a marketing strategy that uses different elements of social media.

Because each social media site offers different features and works in a different way, by making them all work together, you can be sure that you're sharing the audience among each site.

Facebook, for example, gives you much more flexibility than Twitter. It lets you post photos, run groups, and interact with both friends and fans in all sorts of different ways. Dave has thousands of friends and another thousand followers on his Facebook page. By placing his tweets on Facebook and linking to his Twitter account, he's able to share his Twitter content with all of them and give them a reason to follow him on Twitter, too! (See Figure 5.12.)

And this can work the other way, too. If you see someone on Facebook with lots of friends and who tweets, follow him or her on Twitter, and comment on his or her Facebook page. There's a

Figure 5.12   Dave's Facebook page is a busy place, and sometimes he cross-promotes his Twitter account. Each time he does, he gains additional followers.

good chance that the person will follow you back and his or her friends and followers will want to check you out as well.

PUT YOUR TWITTER NAME IN YOUR SIGNATURE

Such an easy thing to do, such an old idea, and so often forgotten.

As soon as a new technology comes along, there can be a tendency to forget about all the old standards, like the value of including your uniform resource locator (URL) on your business card and your e-mail and forum signatures.

Just as that strategy can drive plenty of interested people to your website, adding your Twitter username to those signatures can have exactly the same effect.

Here's Dave's standard e-mail signature:

Dave Taylor

Digital Storyteller

http://www.askdavetaylor.com || @DaveTaylor

And here's Joel's signature:

Joel Comm Author, Speaker, Entrepreneur, Consultant

Tel: 657-200-5635

http://www.Joelcomm.com @JoelComm

Twitter might let you search your contact list for people who are already Twittering, and it might let you send those who aren't on the site an invitation to join up. But if all you want to do is alert people on your e-mail list, people in forums, and anyone else you chat with online that you're Twittering, then this is a very simple way to do it.

RUN A CONTEST

One way to build up followers is to reward them for following you. We also saw that some Twitterers are doing that by giving them a freebie as soon as they hit the *Follow* button.

Another way is to include discount codes in the tweets to keep people reading.

OneKontest (www.onekontest.com) has built a business around managing Twitter-based contests and has clients such as Music Television (MTV), Starbucks, Samsung, Nintendo, and Vodafone.

Consider the *Student Pocket Guide*, a popular digital publication for college students in the United Kingdom. To keep things lively, it's constantly running Twitter giveaways and sweepstakes. In fact, usually people only have to retweet or respond to a message to be entered in the competition. How easy is that?

The latest giveaway? A really cool quadcopter (see Figure 5.13).

The big advantage of competitions like this is that they're happening in real time. The company could just as easily have asked the question on its blog or its Facebook page and said that it would be announcing the winners a week later.

Figure 5.13 The *Student Pocket Guide* (@TheSPG) runs contests on Twitter to keep its followers reading and to make sure that all of its customers follow its tweets.

By running the contest live, through Twitter, it collects all of its customers together in one place at one time, turns them into a community, and creates a party atmosphere, too.

Of course, it also makes sure that all of the publication's customers are following its tweets.

Klout and Page Rank

There are all sorts of different strategies that you can use to build up your follower list. But the number next to your follower list is just one measure of success on Twitter.

No less important is the extent to which you are the focus of conversation.

Because Twitter is like a giant open chat, the more people who reply to your tweets, the more influential your posts become. It's a great sign that people are interested in what you have to say and want to take part in the discussion.

That's the theory, at least, behind one of the measures that the popular ranking site Klout (www.klout.com) uses to give you a relative ranking of your engagement in the social media world. (See Figure 5.14.)

The theory is similar to Google's search engine–based page rank formula, which rates the importance of websites based, among other things, on the number and quality of incoming links the site receives.

Klout lets you see your own score, and you can toss in the usernames of other Twitterers to see their scores, too.

The real question, of course, is how useful this stuff is. The service was created primarily for fun. Unlike Google's page rank, Klout isn't going to affect where you turn up in search results or how much traffic you're likely to receive.

It certainly won't affect the amount of money you receive in advertising revenues or product sales.

You might consider it one way to measure how well you're managing to motivate discussions in comparison with other people in the social media sphere. You can also look at the top 50 Klout scorers to see what they're doing on Twitter and other

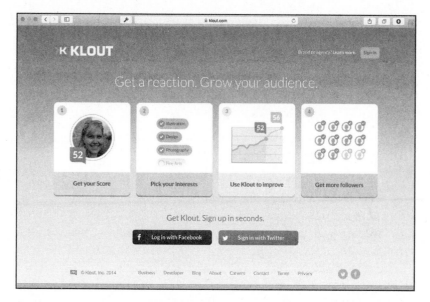

Figure 5.14   Klout is an interesting place to get a sense of how your social media efforts are paying off in visibility and importance.

social media sites to get those replies coming in. Interestingly, though, tweets also receive page ranks.

Consider the search shown in Figure 5.15: the second match in the 4.7 million Google results is a tweet by Neal Schaffer (@NealSchaffer). A tweet is number two out of 4.7 million!

Creating a long list of followers is always going to be one of the most important tasks that you do on Twitter. It's a challenge that requires first deciding what kind of followers you want—an audience that's niched and mostly targeted, one that's large but general, or a balanced combination of the two.

It will then involve a great deal of following and reading. You'll have to reply to tweets that other people have posted, place tweets of your own, and track down the people you know—and would like to know—on the site.

It's a process that takes time. Although there are strategies to make that process faster—and we discussed several of them in this chapter—no one ever builds a four-, five-, or six-figure follower list overnight.

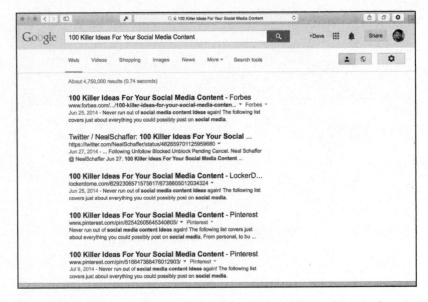

Figure 5.15   Tweets rank on Google and make it into the search results, too.

That's because, above all, creating a large following on Twitter requires writing good tweets—the kind that people actually want to read and that make them feel that you're going to have more good information for them in the future.

That's what we'll explore in the next chapter.

6

The Art of the Tweet

The moment it became clear that the Internet could be a good way for businesses to make money, one simple rule stood out.

Sites with good content succeeded; sites with poor content failed.

That didn't mean that lots of people didn't try earning money with poor content. They did. They still do.

And they still fail.

Sure, a website owner can find a wordsmith in Mumbai to churn out articles for $5 each so that he or she can have somewhere to put his or her ads, but even at those low rates, the owner is still going to lose money.

If the content isn't good, no one will want to read it.

Instead of putting effort into creating good articles, the publisher will have to put even more effort into dragging people to his or her Web pages.

And he or she will have to keep doing it because when users have visited a poor site once, they won't come back.

That rule holds true on Twitter, too.

To build followers and keep them engaged, you have to produce good content.

The only difference is in the nature of good content on Twitter.

Because you have only 140 characters, you can't create long list posts that are so popular in social media sites.

You can't create in-depth how-to articles that give people valuable knowledge and help them complete important tasks.

And any interviews you wanted to run would have to consist of very short questions and one-word answers.

Good content on Twitter needs to be entertaining. It needs to be informative. It needs to be valuable.

And it needs to be short.

In this chapter, we're going to look at some of the ways to produce great Twitter content, the kind of tweets that build followers, keep your readers coming back for more, and engage them in your conversation.

Let's start by talking about the rules.

Tweet Etiquette

Every conversation has rules. We know not to interrupt people when they're talking. We know not to use bad language when we talk. We know not to talk too loudly.

And we know how and when to break all of the rules.

The same is true for a Twitter conversation. Twitter has its own etiquette, just as other social media sites have their own generally agreed-upon network etiquette, or netiquette.

Some of those etiquette rules are smart, are sensible, and should always be followed. Others are smart, are sensible, and should usually be followed.

Although it's important to know the rules, it's just as important then to know when to break them and what happens when you do.

DON'T SPAM

This is one rule you can't break. Spammers don't survive for long on Twitter. They don't build followers. Any followers they do get don't read their tweets, and the number of conversions spammers can generate will be so tiny that, as a marketing method, you'd be better off printing a thousand flyers, folding them into paper airplanes, and tossing them out your office window.

There are all sorts of different ways to spam on Twitter.

As we've seen, one way is to follow lots and lots of people in the hope that some of them will follow you in return. That's not just ineffective, but it's also immediately obvious when someone views your Twitter profile.

Whenever someone's bio shows that he or she is following several thousand people but only being followed by a handful, that's a good sign that he or she is looking to spam. He or she is trying to build up followers who will follow him or her out of politeness rather than because of interesting content.

All smart Twitter users try to avoid people like that.

The spamming itself, though, is done by constantly sending out tweets that say things like "I've just published a new blog post—check it out!" or "Sign up for my feed!" or "Make $100 in the next hour. Here's how . . ."

You can send out tweets like this occasionally. But as we'll see later in this section, they have to be mixed in with other tweets, too. Remember our conversation about like me, know me, trust me, and pay me? Jumping right to pay me can mark you as a spammer and will be quickly ignored, whether you have a dozen followers or 10,000.

Another method popular with spammers is to add popular hashtags or keywords associated with trending topics to their tweets, even if those topics aren't relevant. Although that will bring in plenty of eyeballs, it's also a very quick way to get your timeline closed down.

Spamming isn't just bad manners; it's also terrible marketing.

FOLLOW STYLE RULES

Twitter's founders may have had mobile phones in mind when they designed the service, and plenty of users may be typing their updates from their smartphones, but Twitter still isn't the same as short message service (SMS) messaging.

That means the language needs to look more like real words than the usual SMS-style abbreviations.

For example, typing in uppercase letters looks like you're shouting, and you should always endeavor to spell out words and avoid using numbers instead of letters whenever possible. (So *late* is not spelled *l8*, and *to* is two letters, not a single digit.)

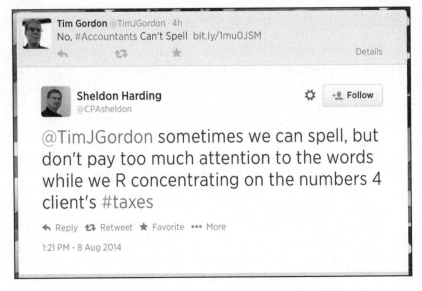

Figure 6.1 Sheldon Harding explains that his lack of style is because he's busy focusing on the bottom line *4* his accounting clients.

That might mean more typing, but the reasoning is sensible. "Heading 2 town 18. Dont no wot 4" is hard for the reader to understand. It's only good manners—and good marketing sense—for you to put in the work so that your readers don't have to.

There are exceptions, of course. If you're really stuck for space, then this is a rule you can break, but understand that you're forcing your followers to expend more effort to understand your message.

What is commonly accepted is to use symbols, such as @ and =, and to skip some of the grammar. The question Twitter asks might be "What are you doing?" but you don't have to begin your answer by saying, "I am . . ." (See Figure 6.1.)

Sentence fragments, such as "Big big soccer match about to start. Can't wait! Go Galaxy!!" are just fine.

Give Credit for Retweets

One of the things that makes Twitter such a powerful tool is the fact that information placed on the site can quickly go viral. When one person spots a good tweet, he or she can pass that message on to followers, and soon it's spreading across the Twitterverse and beyond.

> You'll hear the phrase *go viral* quite often. It just means that it's caught the attention of people, and they're sharing it with their friends. The more that happens, the more popular it becomes. Like a virus. But good.

For a marketer, that's like hitting the jackpot.

On Twitter, it's done by retweeting.

Twitter users can simply copy someone else's tweet and tweet it themselves—but they give credit to the original Twitterer by adding *RT* or *Retweet* together with the username of the original Twitterer. At the moment, the format for retweets then looks like this:

RT @username: original tweet.

Say you wanted to retweet this post from Dave's Twitter account:

Saw the TMNT movie and, well, it's the same movie yet again. Same story. Same jokes. Nothing new, nothing really fun about it. Meh.

You would either click the little *Retweet* link under the tweet (see Figure 6.2) or manually enter the tweet:

RT @DaveTaylor Saw the TMNT movie and, well, it's the same movie yet again. Same story. Same jokes. Nothing new, nothing really fun about it. Meh.

Any comments you want to add to the retweet can go at the beginning or in brackets at the end, as space permits:

I LOVED IT! RT @DaveTaylor Saw the TMNT movie and, well, it's the same movie yet again. Same story. Same jokes. Nothing new . . . Meh.

Figure 6.2 Pay attention to all the handy links under each tweet: *Reply, Retweet, Favorite,* and *More.*

The etiquette is simple enough, but not everyone uses brackets or places personal comments in the right place, so it's not always easy to see what's comment and what's part of the original tweet. And as a tweet spreads across Twitter—when a retweet is retweeted—the original Twitter user can become lost.

That's why Twitter recommends you use that *Retweet* button, as shown in Figure 6.2. That places the tweet on your home page for all your followers to see, too, even if they're not following the person you're retweeting. The tweet will look like any other message, complete with avatar, so the identity of the original Twitterer is clear. (See Figure 6.3.) But it also says who retweeted it so that you know someone you follow sent it. You will be able to retweet the message in turn or reply to it. Very easy.

The value of sharing tweets is easy to understand. It might not be original content, but if your followers would find the original tweet interesting, why shouldn't you share it?

The tricky bit is to get other people to retweet for you, and there's a whole bunch of things you can do to increase the chances that will happen. We'll talk about those a little later in this book, but for now bear in mind that if your tweets are interesting

> **Tweets**   Tweets and replies
>
> 🔁 Retweeted by Joel & Dave
> **Dave Taylor** @DaveTaylor · 39m
> Saw the TMNT movie and, well, it's the same movie yet again. Same
> story. Same jokes. Nothing new, nothing really fun about it. Meh.
>
> ↩   ↻ 1   ★   •••

Figure 6.3 Here's what a proper retweet looks like, complete with
carefully retaining the identity of the original Twitter user who sent
the message.

enough, people will share them with their friends and followers—
and those friends and followers will come to your page to find out
who you are.

STICK TO 140 CHARACTERS

You *have* to stick to 140 characters, right? That's all they give you,
and they do it for a good reason. Being starved of space stops your
waffling and sparks your creativity. It's what Twitter is all about.

Well, yes and no.

Twitter gives you 140 characters because that's all that can fit
through SMS systems. If mobile phone companies could handle
messages of 200 characters, then that's probably how long our
tweets would be.

Even though the limit is arbitrary, it does make sense to keep
to it as much as possible.

The alternative is to show half-complete tweets and offer links
for people to continue reading or break messages up so that
they're sent over several tweets. There are even services such as
TwitLonger (www.twitlonger.com) that allow people to post
messages as long as they like, with the first 140 characters
appearing as a tweet.

You can see all of these things happening sometimes on
Twitter, and they rarely look good. Readers expect the content
on Twitter to be succinct. They expect to be able to read and

absorb it in one bite. These are content snacks, sound bites, not three-course meals with coffee.

Writing a thought that takes more than 140 characters and spreading it over three or four tweets is almost always giving people more than they want. It also makes you look like you're dominating the conversation.

Chat with a friend, and you'll take turns speaking. You'll speak, your friend will respond, and then you'll continue. Keep talking without giving your friend a chance to offer his or her thoughts or reaction, and you'll start to sound rude.

Multiple tweets can have the same effect on Twitter.

Again, this doesn't mean you should *never* break up a long tweet. And it certainly doesn't mean that you shouldn't post one tweet after another if that's the only way to get the message across.

What it does mean is that you should be aware of the impact it can have on your timeline when you do either of these.

FOLLOW PEOPLE WHO FOLLOW YOU

How many people you should follow on Twitter can always make for a great discussion point. Follow thousands of people and you're not going to be able to read all of their tweets. Inevitably, you'll miss tweets you'd really like to read, and you'll look like someone who has lots of acquaintances but no real friends.

When Joel started using Twitter, for example, he followed almost everyone who followed him. The idea was that in giving everyone the benefit of the doubt, he would meet many new people and enter into discussions that he might otherwise have missed. Even then, more were following him than he was following back, so he invariably missed a lot of tweets. Still, it was great to look at Twitter and see a huge variety of different conversations taking place.

It was a bit like strolling through the networking room during a break at a conference. Joel could choose which conversations to join and which to ignore. Valuable, but impossible to follow everyone back.

As his numbers have grown Joel has had to reevaluate his follow strategy on Twitter. With tens of thousands of followers, it became impossible to use Twitter without it becoming a huge time sink and eating up the entire day! Because one of his key reasons for using Twitter has always been to have it fit into his lifestyle, Joel finally took a radical step and unfollowed everyone. He started over. You can read more about why Joel purged his Twitter account, upsetting a few people, but ultimately making his Twitter experience more valuable, at www.comm.us/unfollow.

Dave's used a different strategy, where he has always invited people to follow him on Twitter but has been candid that he follows only people and Twitter accounts that he finds interesting. That's how he follows fewer than 900 people but has thousands of followers. It means that Dave will have conversations with fewer people, but they will be more frequent and meaningful. You might want—at least at the beginning—to reward everyone who follows you by following them in return. Plenty of top Twitterers do this.

If you do, however, at least take a few seconds to ensure that you're not following bots or spammers who have zero followers other than you.

Similarly, you might prefer to follow only close friends and people you already know. That could make you look a bit antisocial, which is not necessarily the best image for a marketer, but it's possible. It just means that the people you follow are "the few, the proud."

Ultimately, this is one place where eventually you have to skip the etiquette and do what works for you. As your follower list grows, you'll have to start being a little bit choosier about whom you follow in return, and your followers will just have to understand that you're being selective, not rude.

Spend any time on Twitter and you're going to come across plenty of other rules, too. Some purists, for example, have argued that your tweets should describe only what you're doing, not what you're thinking or planning to do. We think that's far too restrictive, and judging by the way that Twitter has developed, other people seem to agree: if a status update sparks a conversation and entertains your followers, it's a fair topic. If people don't like it, they should read someone else's tweets.

And that's really the ultimate test of tweet etiquette: how other people react and how you would react to the same kind of thing.

If you're building followers and they're responding to what you're writing, you're doing the right things. It's as easy as that.

The Benefits of Following before Tweeting

One of the results of flexible Twitter etiquette is that it's inevitable that every Twitterer ends up making and following his or her own rules.

Some Twitterers follow everyone who follows them; others don't.

Some reply to everyone who @replies them; others don't reply to anyone.

Some engage with their followers via direct messages; others ignore all direct messages and are unreachable through that channel.

Some ask questions and expect followers to answer; others never do.

That means before you dive into a conversation—and even before you get your own tweeting career fully under way with regular tweets that spark conversations and market your products and your services—it's important to spend time following others and reading their tweets.

Clearly that's going to take a little time, but the advantages are important.

First, you'll get to see the etiquette rules that they're following. If you can see that someone you'd like to add as a follower has 1,000 followers but follows only 40 people, you shouldn't be too upset if he or she doesn't add you the minute you add him or her.

You'll also see whether he or she thinks using numbers instead of letters is annoying or acceptable (based on whether the person does so) and what he or she likes to tweet about.

No less important, you can investigate and ascertain who's following him or her so that you can follow them, too, and understand who might follow you if you turn this Twitterer into a follower.

But perhaps most crucially, if you spend time following and reading tweets before you dive into a conversation, you'll be able to identify what caused the person to respond to one of his or her followers in the first place.

This is what you want to happen when you tweet directly to other people by hitting the *Reply* button. Your timeline will look as though you're in conversation with all sorts of interesting people. When those users reply to your @replies, your name and a link to your Twitter page appear in their timeline, too. All of their followers can see it and will want to know who you are.

It's fantastic marketing.

By looking at the questions that other repliers asked and the responses they posted, you'll be able to understand what you have to reply—or post—to win that prize.

How to Join a Conversation

One of the things that makes Twitter so appealing is that it's such an open community. There might be millions of people talking about what they're doing and chatting with others, but you really do feel that every one of them could be your friend if you wanted him or her to be.

That's a remarkable feeling, and it's something you can't find on many social media sites. Facebook, for example, requires a potential friend to confirm that he or she knows you before you can even see the person's profile, let alone add him or her as a contact.

Twitter is much more communal. Most everyone on the site seems to be available to provide information, swap a tip, or hand over some valuable piece of advice.

On one condition: you give him or her something valuable in return.

That means when you want to take part in a conversation that you see on Twitter, you can't simply introduce yourself and expect to be welcomed.

Twitter might feel like a giant room full of people networking and making connections, but it doesn't work the same way.

If other people on the site want to know who you are, they can stop by your profile, read your bio, and surf through to your website.

What they really want to know is what you have to contribute to the discussion.

And that can't be a plug for you, your products, or your business.

Or rather, it can't *just* be a plug for you.

If all you do is say something like "I covered this topic in my blog! Check it out here: tinyurl.com/xyzzy," then you're going to sound like a salesperson and alienate people almost instantly.

If, on the other hand, you provide some solid information that you drew out of that post *and* provide a link to a place where readers can learn more, then you're paying for the return reply.

Do you see the difference?

The first type of tweet is an ad; the second type is a contribution to the conversation.

But you don't have to do anything as blatant as including a link in your tweet to get the benefits of joining a conversation if you do it right.

Consider Figure 6.4 for a moment. It's a discussion between Dave's and Nokia's @NokiaUS Twitter accounts, and you read it top to bottom. Nokia announced a new green mobile phone, and Dave immediately responded with a question about the packaging: Is the packaging green, too?

Nokia responded, leading to a discussion between them, a discussion that led directly to Dave gaining new followers, people who looked at the Twitter page for Nokia USA and saw Dave mentioned.

It's a technique that can work only through conversation, but with even a little bit of creativity, it can produce great results.

Note that in Figure 6.4 Dave carefully ensures that he doesn't do an @reply with Nokia, too, in the first tweet by embedding its account name in the middle of the message or in the second by prefixing its handle (@NokiaUS) with a dot. Why? To ensure that the maximum number of people see the back-and-forth.

That's just one way to join a conversation, and as you can see, it's incredibly simple. In fact, you can think of it as a little like a traditional link exchange. The better your tweets and the more

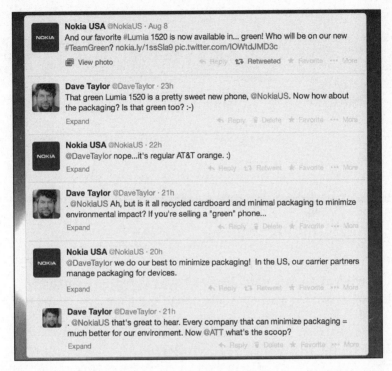

Figure 6.4 Dave and Nokia USA engage in a discussion about green packaging with the new Lumia smartphone.

popular your Twitter page, the easier it's going to be to get your name on other people's timelines.

Providing information isn't the only way to join a conversation, though. An alternative method is to ask for information.

This is another good reason to read someone's timeline before you join the conversation. Some Twitterers are fantastic at answering people's questions. Others aren't so hot. That might be because they don't have the time. It could be because they have too many followers. Or it might just be because that's not what they want to do with their Twitter presence.

Read the old tweets first, and you'll be able to see how often the Twitterer answers and what kind of questions he or she is likely to answer, too. (See Figure 6.5.)

Figure 6.5 Popular author Marsha Collier keeps her community close by answering their questions and offering great feedback, too.

How to Be Interesting on Twitter

This is what it all comes down to. You can follow etiquette, offer great tips in replies to other people's tweets, and ask questions that get your name in the timelines of the most important people on Twitter.

But none of that will mean a thing if you don't have the sort of content and conversations on your timeline that will turn those visitors into followers—and your followers into customers, clients, or regular users.

Even though Twitter asks a very specific question, there's a huge range of different kinds of content that you can write as tweets. In this section, we're going to describe the most important and the most effective kinds of tweets.

In general, you can divide your tweets into two types: broadcasts and conversations.

It should be clear now that Twitter can be used in two ways. One way is to convey information—to tell your followers what you are doing, are thinking, or have been doing until now.

That's a one-way stream. Tweets like these don't generally produce any sort of replies. They're meant to be informative and entertaining, and although people might reply to them, their first function is for you to tell your followers something they don't know.

It's little different from the way that a television station works.

The second type of tweets are those intended to spark discussions or that form a part of a discussion. Questions and answers to other people's questions and replies are obviously conversation tweets, but they can be much subtler than that. Just tweeting something controversial or even just writing the sort of thing that people will want to know more about can make for a good conversation tweet, too.

And having a conversation brings all sorts of benefits.

We've seen that when people reply to one of your tweets, your name and link appear on their timeline, winning you more followers. Each discussion starter then can act like a viral ad.

You can reply to their replies, giving you easy additional content and an enjoyable conversation.

And the discussion as a whole can help build a community and bring your followers—and potential customers—closer to your brand.

Ideally, a Twitter timeline should contain a good mixture of both kinds of tweets. If you're busy replying and chatting to your followers, you might start to look a little too cliquey. You'll probably find that you'll be talking to the same group of people and, worse, that you won't have complete control over the conversation. Instead of saying what you want to say, you'll feel obligated to discuss the topics that your followers want to talk about, not what you want to discuss.

On the one hand, if that's what you want your timeline to do, that's fine. Lots of people use Twitter in that way—much like a large, open instant messaging board—but if you're using Twitter for marketing, you will want to keep control of the message and the subjects of the discussions.

On the other hand, if all you do is broadcast, then your timeline is going to look a little dull. Although there are some very successful Twitterers who do nothing but broadcast—President Obama's campaign tweeting picked up millions of followers during the election but did little more than tell people which rallies he was addressing—most Twitter users find it pays to combine the two approaches.

Use broadcast tweets to make sure the information you want to share gets across.

And use conversation tweets to turn those followers into a community, keep them coming back, and make sure that the issues they want discussed are addressed.

These are some of the most effective types of tweets that you can send: link, classic, opinion, mission accomplished, entertainment, question, and picture tweets.

LINK TWEETS—"THIS IS WHAT I'M WORKING ON NOW"

This is probably the most common type of broadcast tweet, if only because there are a number of Twitter apps that let bloggers turn their posts into tweets automatically. But it can also be darn effective. (See Figure 6.6.)

If you've put up a new blog post, then you'll want people to know about it and read it, and many of your followers will want to

Figure 6.6   "Read all about what I'm working on now here . . ."

do just that. Digital Photography School (DPS) has a terrific Twitter account, @digitalps, and offers a great example of a tweet that's purely a link to content elsewhere on the Web. (See Figure 6.7.)

Even though this timeline does nothing but automatically announce new posts that have been published on the school's blog, it has 116,000 followers. Even if it has only a 1 percent click-through rate, that's still 1,600 people who will go check out each new article. *For posting a single tweet!*

Now we don't know what their figures really are, but if they're converting 3 percent of site visitors into e-book buyers and generating, say, $4 from each book sold, then each tweet is worth just less than $200 in direct revenue.

Post four to five new entries each day and drive 50 percent new traffic each time, and you could easily be seeing $500 to $1,000 per day in sales directly attributable to Twitter.

To be fair, we doubt that they're generating this much revenue from this Twitter account. One reason is that as follower numbers grow, click-through and conversion rates start to drop even if the overall figures get bigger. There's also a big likelihood that almost all of the people who visit the second link you post also visited the

Figure 6.7   Could DPS's photography tweets be simpler? And yet they're driving traffic and helping produce revenue from the site.

first, and so on. New visitors are the hard currency; new users, that Holy Grail of new customer acquisition.

Still, our scenario demonstrates that it is possible to measure the value of a tweet that links to a website and that the potential for earning with tweets that link to high-earning sites can be very rewarding indeed—especially when it's almost completely effortless.

Once the Twitter account has been opened and the WordPress plug-in installed, all the DPS team has to do is focus on producing great content on its website, and it could be picking up $200 or more in daily revenue.

So, how do you create blog broadcast tweets like these?

The easiest method is to install one of the many Twitter plug-ins directly to your WordPress blog. Once configured, it automatically posts a summary of each new post, along with a shortened link that's Twitter friendly.

We recommend the Jetpack suite of plug-ins from the same development team that helps keep WordPress itself humming along. Start by going to jetpack.me (see Figure 6.8).

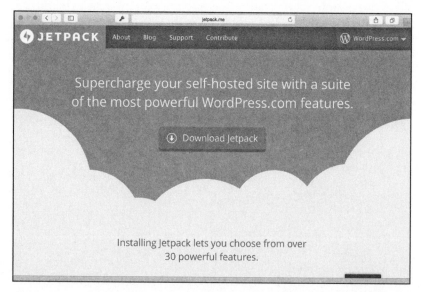

Figure 6.8   Jetpack (jetpack.me) offers a suite of splendid social media tools, including a Twitter feed utility, for any WordPress user.

Take the time to familiarize yourself with the more than 30 different plug-ins and tools that are included in the (free) Jetpack suite; it's quite impressive. The specific plug-in you want is called *Publicize* (see Figure 6.9). It lets you connect your WordPress blog to Facebook, LinkedIn, Tumblr, Path, Google Plus, and, of course, Twitter.

The alternative to using Publicize—or a similar service—is to write the tweets manually. That will give you complete control over when you update, but it will require a little more effort.

There is a risk involved in using this automated method. DPS is interesting enough—and well-known enough—for people to want to follow the automated blog tweets just to stay informed. It's little different from following the blog's really simple syndication (RSS) feed.

But you can't rely on this method if the site doesn't have its own pulling power already. Few people are going to be attracted by a headline from a firm it doesn't know.

Dell, for example, which has made millions of dollars in sales through Twitter-based promotions, has multiple accounts,

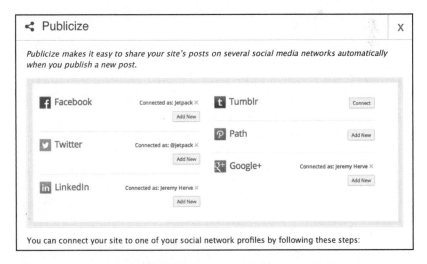

Figure 6.9 The Jetpack Publicize plug-in is a must-install for all WordPress users. And don't forget to connect your Twitter account, too!

Figure 6.10   Giving Joel's followers fun with a link tweet.

allowing each of its business units to target specific markets. Its two primary channels are the business-to-consumer Direct2Dell (@direct2dell) and the enterprise computing Dell Cloud Computing (@dellintheclouds). Much of what you'll see are headlines from that business's blog.

The result is that even a company the size of Dell has an uphill battle trying to gain large followings on each of its Twitter accounts.

Of course, your own blog uniform resource locators (URLs) aren't the only kind of links you can include in your tweets. You can add links to any sites that you've found interesting and, more important, that you think your users would find interesting.

You can even send links to the articles you're reading at the moment or food you're about to eat! (See Figure 6.10.)

This will mean that you're sending people away from your timeline, but they're going to leave anyway. It's much better that they leave with the impression that you're up to date with the latest news on your topic and that you're a source both of great information and of fun distractions.

CLASSIC TWEETS—"THIS IS WHAT I'M DOING NOW"

It's unlikely that you're going to get many replies to link tweets. Your followers will click the link and leave, and by the time they remember they want to tell you what they think of the post, they're already long gone.

You might receive a few replies, but on the whole these are broadcast posts that are intended to be informative rather than updates that you can expect to provoke discussion.

But these could well be the only type of tweets that are purely one-way. As long as your followers are staying on your timeline, there's always the chance that someone will have a comment to make.

That's true even when you write the most basic of tweets—the one that Twitter suggests and that the site was created for: when you tell people what you're doing right now.

These are always going to be among the easiest types of tweets to create, and they're not hard to make interesting. Try to avoid describing what you're eating (unless it's an epic chicken parmesan. Remember earlier when we said it was important to know when to break the rules?). Too many people do this and—unless you're traveling through the Sahara desert and dining on camel meat and roasted scorpions—that's going to get old very quickly. Focus on the various activities that you do during the day.

But here's the thing.

Don't just say, "Heading to the library" or "About to take a nap." *Also say what you think about what you're doing or explain why you're doing it.*

That makes the tweet so much more interesting.

The benefit of these tweets is that they let your followers follow you through the day. That's the idea of Twitter. It's a bit like reality TV, but you can choose from millions of lives to follow instead of the odd people the producers cram into the *Big Brother* house.

Just telling people exactly what you're doing then can be interesting, but talking to your followers about what you're doing is a little like stepping into the video booth and taking them into your confidence. (See Figure 6.11.)

It has a much more powerful binding effect and is far more entertaining.

So a tweet that might have said, "Heading to the library" becomes "Heading to the library to grab two kids' books for E. If I read *The Gruffalo* one more time, my head will explode."

Figure 6.11　Don't just tell us what you're doing; tell us what you think about what you're doing or why you're doing it, too.

And even "About to take a nap" would become "About to take a nap. Fingers already half-asleep. Summertime always does this to me."

Do you see how posts like these add personality to your timeline?

They don't just announce what you're doing. They describe who you are, too. They're the small talk that builds the connections and the trust on which all relationships—including business relationships—are built.

When you're competing for the attention of followers from among millions of other Twitter users, these little details can help you stand out.

OPINION TWEETS—"THIS IS WHAT I'M THINKING NOW"

Okay, Twitter doesn't actually ask what you're thinking, and there are even some Twitter purists who feel that tweets should be only about actions, not opinions. (See Figure 6.12.)

We think they're wrong; that's our shared opinion.

Just as you can make tweets about actions more interesting when you also state your thoughts about those actions, so also you can make your timeline more personal when you include tweets

Figure 6.12   Sheesh . . . it's just an opinion.

that describe what you think or demonstrate a particular political or religious bias.

Anyone who has read Joel's tweets and his blog knows that he's not someone who is afraid to state his opinion. He has lots of them, they're strongly held—and some people don't agree with them.

That's fine. They don't have to read them.

Joel understands that telling people what he thinks about the various issues that concern him might put some people off following him and reading his blog posts.

Heck, it could cost him customers.

But Joel's prepared to accept that and suspects that it's not penalizing him anyway. On the contrary, he's convinced that his openness and the fact that his readers know where he stands and what he thinks—even if they don't always agree—has an overall positive effect. The people he loses by expressing his opinions are made up for by the close connection he has with the readers and followers who remain.

Dave has a similar perspective, though he only rarely delves into politics or religion. But sometimes a personal philosophy of "live and let live" can be overrun by shock and distress over a particular situation or comment someone makes online. Certainly on his fatherhood blog—GoFatherhood.com—and, by extension, his Twitter stream, he shares his views about fatherhood, parenting, and the role of boys and men in contemporary culture, often sparking major debate.

That's always a choice you have to make when expressing an opinion, especially on controversial issues and especially when you're using Twitter for marketing. If you're marketing a corporate brand rather than a personal brand, for example, it's a good idea to keep the opinions focused on topics that affect your industry.

People without opinions look impersonal; companies without opinions look impartial.

If you are using Twitter to reinforce your personal brand, feel free to share your thoughts on anything that comes to mind.

Tell people what you think of something that affects your industry.

Tell them what you think of something that's happening in the news.

Tell them what you think of something someone else posted.

Use tweets to tell people what you think about anything, and you'll be putting your personality into your timeline.

MISSION-ACCOMPLISHED TWEETS—"THIS IS WHAT I'VE JUST DONE"

Share your thoughts and you're almost guaranteed to get people sharing theirs. Few things can start a discussion faster than saying something that you know lots of other people feel strongly about.

Telling people what you've just done can have the same effect. (See Figure 6.13.)

These kinds of tweets look like broadcasts. They're little different from tweets that announce that you've just uploaded a new blog post.

Both talk about activities that you've already completed.

But although your followers can see the results of your link tweets, they won't always be able to see the results of your mission accomplished tweets. They'll only be able to comment on them.

Announcing that "I've just done this" is also another way of saying, "What do you think of this?"

And the result is often answers to a question you didn't know you were asking. That's particularly true when the task you've accomplished is particularly interesting or impressive.

Figure 6.13 Mission accomplished!

Tell people that you just broke $1,000 in monthly AdSense earnings, for example, and you can be confident that one of your followers will congratulate you—and ask you how you did it.

Tell them you just powered up a level in World of Warcraft, and you could get a similar response.

And tell them that you've just baked a chocolate cake and that you're about to get stuck in with a cup of coffee and the newspaper, and you'll probably get people asking you if they could have some, too.

Tweeting about what you've done might be an odd way to answer the question "What are you doing now?" but it can be a very good way to fill your timeline and pique the interest of your followers.

ENTERTAINMENT TWEETS—"I'M MAKING YOU LAUGH NOW"

Followers follow people whose tweets they find informative, but they also follow people whose tweets they find entertaining. Stephen Fry's tweets, for example, are filled with the sorts of witty comments and insights that gave him a career as a comedy actor. Reading them is like watching one of his television shows—in 140-character bites.

If you can come up with tweets that are fun and entertaining to read, as well as genuinely helpful, then you'll never struggle to find followers. (See Figure 6.14.)

Ideally, of course, all of your tweets would be filled with jokes, humor, or wit. If you can't manage that, though, then depending on the subject of your timeline—and your ability to crack jokes— tossing in the odd humorous tweet can help lighten the mood and make your Twitter page something amusing to follow. You'll be the life of the digital party, one tweet at a time.

Figure 6.14 Okay, so Joel sometimes has bizarre thoughts . . .

QUESTION TWEETS—"CAN YOU HELP ME DO SOMETHING NOW?"

One very easy way to turn your followers from readers into contributors is to ask a question. Smart Twitter users do this all the time, tossing out requests for help from anyone in their follower list who might have some good advice.

Often, the questions will be very simple—ideas for birthday presents, recipes for tonight's dinner, and so on. Sometimes, they can be complex and demand expert help from people with specialized knowledge. Other times it's as simple as a request for a new band to audition, a new book, or even a new TV show to binge watch. (See Figure 6.15.)

But questions don't just have to be requests for information. They can also be discussion starters. Ask your followers what they think about a topic, and you'll soon know just how engaged your followers really are—especially if you throw in your opinion first.

Tweeting, "I can't stand violent video games" could get a discussion started in response.

Tweeting, "What do you think of violent video games?" could have a similar effect.

But getting the discussion rolling by tweeting, "My son plays violent video games. I can't stand them. What do you think?"

Figure 6.15 Musician Jackson Harris puts out a call for suggestions from his followers.

increases the chances that your followers will hit the *Reply* button and toss in their two cents.

Picture Tweets—"Look at What I've Been Doing"

The short text updates that Twitter offers make both reading and contributing quick, letting users dip in and out. The investment in time and effort is small, but the rewards can be much, much bigger.

Not surprisingly, Twitterers have been looking for ways around those restrictions. Including a link that takes the follower to a website is one simple way to do that, but you can also add a picture to your tweets.

There are two ways to do this. If you're using an app, such as Instagram, you can have it send out a tweet to your followers with a link to a photo you just posted. Not so exciting. Actually use Twitter to create the tweet and include or attach a photo, however, and it shows up in the Twitter stream for all your followers. Far superior.

Including a photo is a great way to draw attention to your content, as demonstrated in Figure 6.16. Remember that old adage about words being only worth 1/1,000 of a picture . . .

In theory, you can do this any way you want. There's no reason why you couldn't post an image to your Flickr stream, then add the link to a tweet, but we recommend using Twitter directly to ensure that the photo itself ends up embedded in the Twitter stream.

It's very neat, very simple, and a very good way to share one more type of information with your followers.

Other Types of Tweets

As we look back on our own tweets, both of us can see that many of them can be easily categorized based on what's discussed in this chapter, but not all. This list isn't exhaustive, but it can supply you with models of the various kinds of tweets that you might want to include in your timeline. Think of it as brainstorming, for a place

Eric Elkins
@datingdad

⚙ ·👤 Follow

Indeed. RT @CousinDangereux: Now this,
THIS is an aisle.

↩ Reply 🔁 Retweet ★ Favorite ••• More

FAVORITES
2

2:15 PM - 9 Aug 2014   Flag media

Figure 6.16   Eric Elkins retweets (that's what the *RT* means) a photo
from @CousinDangereux, also neatly demonstrating the viral effect of
Twitter.

to turn when you think, "I have no idea what I should be talking
about on Twitter to build up my following!"

Let's have a look . . .

The Mundane

Full of self-absorption and without any apparent redeeming value,
the mundane tweet is the backbone of Twitter. Narcissistic and
banal, it's "all about me." But don't think for a second that the
mundane tweet is not without merit. On the contrary, it's those
mundane tweets that help build the foundations of a relationship.
They're the first two steps that take you from *Like me* and *Know
me* to *Trust me* and *Pay me*.

Here's a typical mundane tweet: "In the New Zealand Air lounge at Sydney airport. Nice digs. Waiting for flight to SFO."

In fact, Joel had already released the highly successful *Twitter Power*, first edition, before the true impact of the mundane tweet really settled in.

His mundane tweet was a photo of two donuts with the accompanying text "What's your favorite donut? Make mine chocolate!" and the overwhelming level of engagement Joel received in response that really opened his eyes to the value of mundane.

The reason is this: mundane tweets provide more points of commonality with others than something more specific provides. Regardless of your preference for glazed or cream filled, donuts are something that the vast majority of us can identify with.

When you talk about something that your followers can identify with, it humanizes you more in their eyes. In Joel's case, posting about donuts helped others see him as a regular guy and not just a *New York Times* best-selling author. Authenticity wins again.

The Communicator

Instant messaging is mostly for person-to-person communication. Forums allow more people to enter the conversation, but the process is slow. The immediacy of Twitter has facilitated dialog in a completely new way. Not only can you respond to someone else's tweet instantly, but also, others can enter the discussion just as easily. The communicator tweet is nothing more than a public reply to another member. Many of the relationships formed via Twitter find their roots in this simple interactive tweet.

This is a typical communicator tweet: "@nprscottsimon, remind me, what's the difference between the NPR and @ifart app again?;-)"

The Answerman

The answerman tweet can be as simple as responding to a trivia question or as serious as helping someone locate a dry cleaner in New York City. If you are able to answer a question for someone, why not lend a hand? It's instant recognition for you and a big help to him or her.

This is a typical answerman tweet: "Check out @omNovia Web Conference. DM me and I can answer some of your questions, too.:-)"

The Sage

Want to tweet but don't have anything particularly important to say? Looking for something more significant than "Watching *Three Stooges* reruns. Gosh I love Curly!"?

Simply find a quote from a famous author, lyrics from a favorite song, or a line from a classic film to share with your followers. Pithy sayings and little tidbits of information are always a useful and entertaining way to keep your timeline ticking over—and they often get retweeted, too.

Here's a typical sage tweet: "'Only passions, great passions, can elevate the soul to great things.' —Denis Diderot"

The Reporter

Twitter has made citizen journalists out of all of us. From the terrorist attacks in Mumbai and the US Airways plane going down in the Hudson to the election sham in Iran and the death of Michael Jackson, more people are getting breaking news on Twitter than anywhere else. If you've got news—accurate news, of course—why not share it and inform your followers?

This is a typical reporter tweet: "Just heard that jazz legend Charlie Haden died. Stinks. Love his musical style. You'll be missed, Charlie. R.I.P."

The Kudos

Giving compliments is a fantastic way to show appreciation for someone. It's even more impactful when done on Twitter because it's a public forum. Not only does the person or business receive the kudos, but all of your followers also see it.

Here's a typical kudos tweet: "My wife just looks stunning today. I've still got a huge crush on her. <3."

The Critic

Some people just love to criticize—and sometimes that can be a good thing, especially on Twitter, where companies are watching for negative comments.

This is a typical critic tweet: "United lost my luggage. Again. Surprise, surprise."

The Advocate

Every Friday on Twitter is FollowFriday, the day when Twitterers recommend that their followers follow selected people they follow. Just add the hashtag #followfriday or even #FF to your tweet, and list the usernames of the people you're recommending. Don't recommend more than about half a dozen people at a time, though; otherwise the introduction loses its shine. And, of course, you don't have to wait until Friday to do this.

Figure 6.17 shows a typical advocate tweet.

The Benefactor

People love free stuff. They also enjoy winning things. The benefactor tweet is used for contests or giveaways. Designed to be

Figure 6.17 Encourage people to follow your team or friends with #FF or #FollowFriday.

retweeted, the goal is have your tweet go viral so that more people are aware of your contest. The benefactor tweet is known to receive many retweets and can help increase your follower count quickly and legitimately.

This is a typical benefactor tweet: "I'm giving away the 4th edition of AdSense Secrets for FREE! No strings attached. http:// adsense-secrets.com"

VARY THE KINDS OF TWEETS YOU USE

Twitter asks a very simple question, and the answers it receives to that question have turned it into an Internet phenomenon. But one of the reasons that the site managed to expand so quickly is that its users have expanded the scope of its activities, too.

Top Twitterers don't just explain what they're doing now. They also reveal what they've *been* doing, what they would like to do, and what they're thinking as well. They make their followers laugh, think, read, and above all, respond—and they do it with different kinds of tweets.

In this section, we've described some of the tweets that we both use to keep our followers engaged and some of the tweets that we've seen other Twitterers using to good effect, too.

You don't have to use all of these different kinds of tweets. On the whole, though, you're going to get the best results when you mix things up.

That should give you a social atmosphere in which you're the host and free to make announcements and share your news.

There is one type of tweet that you *shouldn't* post, though: the kind of tweet that gets you in trouble.

We've all heard about people who have created videos of themselves doing stupid things, then posted them on YouTube for everyone—including their boss—to see.

The same thing can happen on Twitter.

Consider public relations (PR) executive Justine Sacco, who posted what she thought was an ironic, humorous tweet just before she boarded a flight from London to South Africa (see Figure 6.18).

Figure 6.18 Justine Sacco's PR career imploded from this single tweet from late December 2013.

As you can imagine, there was universal outrage, and by the time she landed in Cape Town, she had been fired from her agency and was the talk of the Twitterverse, to the point where journalists actually met her airplane and interviewed her on the spot, much to her astonishment (and chagrin).

Twitter may sometimes feel like a private space in which you're just shooting the breeze with your pals, but it's not. People read it, law enforcement agencies monitor it, and everything you tweet is in the public record forever, so if there's anything you don't want everyone and his or her uncle to know, don't tweet it.

There are plenty of other ways to write enticing tweets without landing yourself in hot water!

How to Drive Behavior

So far we've been focusing largely on one particular type of follower response to your tweets. Although some tweets simply provide information, others will spark a discussion in which your followers will provide information of their own in return, spreading your name across the Twitterverse and giving you a community.

But sometimes you want your followers to do other things.

Usually, that means clicking a link, but it rarely stops there. Once your followers have reached the website, you'll need to do something to monetize them or at least start the process of monetizing them.

Your ability to do that will clearly depend far more on what that website says than on what a 140-character tweet says, but what you say on Twitter can have an effect on what the follower does eventually. Especially if you write the right kind of tweets.

We've already seen, for example, how the *Palo Alto Weekly* gets its users not just to visit its site but also to make purchases by sharing a discount code.

Discount cards and time-limited offers are just two classic ways that you can influence follower behavior, though.

Another method is to use spontaneity. Because Twitter happens in real time, you can decide to interact with your followers spontaneously.

Anyone who's following your tweets at that particular moment gets to join in the fun and feel the benefits.

People who stop by later will feel that they missed an opportunity and realize that they should be reading your tweets more often.

When followers understand that this is a one-off surprise chance to pick up some valuable information, there's a good chance that they'll tune in.

Ultimately, though your tweets can create interest, excitement, and anticipation, they can only do so much. The real conversion work comes when followers reach your Web page, which is why you must have your sales channels ready and set up before you drive your followers toward them.

But direct sales aren't the only way you can benefit from a long list of engaged followers. In the next chapter, we'll look at what interacting with your customers can do for you.

7

The Magic of Connecting with Customers on Twitter

When you produce interesting tweets, your followers benefit.

They find their way to your site, where they can pick up valuable information.

They enjoy the benefits of special offers and discount codes.

They gain a greater understanding of the sort of products, services, and information you provide.

They feel part of a community that shares even more useful information and that provides support, too.

They can have a good time as well.

But a solid group of followers is also a resource for you, and not just because some of those followers will go ahead and make purchases either from you or from your sponsors. They're valuable because they're a giant source of information.

They're a source of information about your market and your products.

They're a source of information about who's talking about you, spreading your name, and winning you referrals.

And they're a source of information about all sorts of things that can help you improve your products and grow your business.

In this chapter, we're going to explain how Twitter users are using the site to build a focus group of customers that they can draw on to increase their bottom line.

Identifying Problems and Soliciting Feedback

The people who choose to follow you on Twitter are your most dedicated customers. They're the ones who want to be the first to know when you release a new product. They want to know what you're planning next, to pick up discounts that will cut the cost of their next purchase, and to lend you a hand, too.

Many of your followers will be such enthusiasts that they'll want to have an influence over your products, your blog posts, or the direction of your company.

They want to contribute.

All you have to do is take advantage of that offer of help.

One way to do that is to give your followers a sneak peek before a major release and ask what they think. (See Figure 7.1.)

Your followers will love this. They'll see that they're being told about a new product before anyone else, and it'll make them feel like part of an exclusive club.

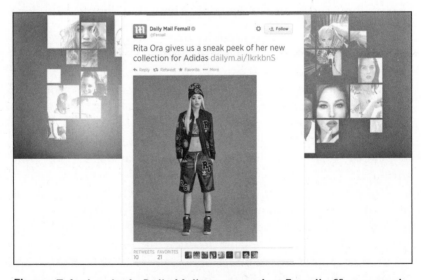

Figure 7.1 London's *Daily Mail* newspaper's @Femail offers a sneak peek at singer Rita Ora's new clothing line for Adidas.

When they tweet you back with their comments, you'll get to identify problems, bugs, and areas of improvement before you take the product public. You'll also get to build up interest so that when you do hit the release date, you've already primed the market, and you'll be able to use their praise as testimonials that you can include on your sales page.

Oh, and they'll retweet and share it like mad, too. Because then it makes them seem like insiders with special knowledge and access, just as Dave, who is a film critic, constantly shares with his followers the films he's going to see before their official release dates.

When business book writer Susan Page was approached by her publisher to update one of her books, she turned to the Twitter community for feedback and suggestions about what to add (see Figure 7.2.)

What she could also have done is set up a mailing list where she pointed her Twitter followers so that they'd receive an announcement when the book is published. Perhaps with a special fan discount of some sort included in that message, as we've discussed earlier in the book. That's very simple. You don't

Figure 7.2 Writer Susan Page (@powerofbpi) puts her followers to work to help her with the new edition of her business process book.

have to do any more than make what you want examined available and then send out a tweet. You'll get a ton of very valuable feedback.

But this is another time to remember that Twitter is a public forum. When your followers hit the *Reply* button to tell you what they think, they're also going to be telling both the rest of your followers and their followers what they think.

That could be valuable marketing. It will help spread the word about your launch or new product or service. But that word-of-mouth marketing is going to be helpful only if your product is almost ready to go (or is already launched). If you need to make a lot of corrections before you release your product, then that second group of followers is going to potentially see a lot of criticism and very little praise. That's not likely to lead to sales.

If the product you want feedback about is almost ready, then ask your followers to reply. Everyone will then see the responses.

If you think the product or the sales page might still need a lot of work, ask followers to direct message or e-mail you. You won't get the viral marketing, but you will get some valuable, relatively confidential feedback.

The drawback to inviting feedback in this way is that any comments you receive are likely to be succinct. If you're asking people to reply, they're not going to do more than identify one or two elements that could be changed and point them out in 140 characters or fewer.

If you're asking them to e-mail you, you might get a longer message, but, to be frank, you're still not likely to get a huge amount of detail. Your followers will want to be helpful, but few of them are going to invest a huge amount of time into improving your product or your sales copy.

Unless you ask them a heap of detailed questions.

Consider the credit reporting company Happy Mango. As it was ready to move into the beta release of its product, it not only wanted to get feedback from users but also wanted to incentivize people to try the product, too. All neatly done in a single tweet, as you can see in Figure 7.3.

As a method of generating detailed feedback as well as increased marketing range, surveys can be very powerful. And

Figure 7.3 Happy Mango invites followers to take their survey and offers a $10 gift card for the hassle. Smart!

the benefit of offering a free download, a free report, or even a gift card or product credit can be a great motivator for followers who share your tweets and gain you more visibility and—hopefully!—more customers.

Discovering Your Top Fans, Promoters, and Evangelists

Read someone's Twitter timeline and it's going to feel a little like walking into a private party. The Twitterer will be posting his or her own content, sharing personal thoughts and what he or she is doing, replying to followers, and addressing issues that others have raised.

There should be plenty of other interesting content there, too, but much of the timeline of a good Twitterer will be directed at individuals, engaging in that all-important dialog.

But when you consider the huge number of people interacting on Twitter, you should always be asking the question "Why those individuals?" How do Twitter users choose which people to engage, which to mention specifically, and which to ignore?

How *should* they choose them?

> MediaBistro reports that Starbucks is mentioned in 10 Tweets *per second* on Twitter. There's no way the company can keep up, even with a team of dedicated social media marketers on staff. In fact, there are three people on the Starbucks Twitter team as of this writing: Archana, Jeremy, and Madeline, all based at Starbucks's headquarters in Seattle, Washington.

Often, a reply that drops a name in front of every other follower on a list will be a direct response to something that Twitter user said. Hit *reply* to a tweet, and there's a good chance that the Twitterer will hit *reply* back. That's especially true if you've done your homework, read the timeline, and paid attention to the sorts of things that might catch his or her attention.

Spot that someone you follow tends to reply to questions, for example, and you should then get a response to a thoughtful or witty query. If he or she responds to praise, then a pat on the back could win you a place on his or her timeline.

But there's another reason that you could—and should— mention one of your followers: if that follower is one of your fans, evangelists, or key marketers.

Every good business has people like this. They're your most loyal customers, the ones who rave about your products to their friends, send links to your articles to their contact list, and are always getting in touch with questions, suggestions, and feedback.

Those people are worth gold to any business, and every good marketer will want to do everything he or she can both to keep them happy and to make the most of them.

Twitter lets you do both. It helps you to find them, too.

In fact, there are all sorts of ways to discover who is talking about you the most on Twitter—and companies are using them.

Dave reviews a lot of different software and hardware for his popular AskDaveTaylor.com blog, and smart vendors pay attention and respond, as shown in Figure 7.4.

The company had been alerted to its name in a tweet and responded by following a tech expert who had positive things to say about its flagship software product. Smart.

Figure 7.4   Dave likes Wide Angle Software's Tune Sweeper, and the company responds by thanking him—and following him on Twitter.

But how do you keep track of mentions of your company, your executives, your products, and yourself?

One method is simply to toss your username or search pattern into Twitter's search engine at search.twitter.com or in the search field on your Twitter page and see what comes up. You will be able to see who has mentioned you and respond as desired (see Figure 7.5).

The search will tell you who has been talking about you in the past only. Unless you leave it open in your browser and refresh the page constantly, it won't alert you to who is talking about you now.

Twitter has a variety of ways you can do this, but don't be confused by Twitter Alerts, which are a way for you to get emergency information from organizations, such as the Federal Emergency Management Administration (FEMA), which you can receive by going to twitter.com/fema/alerts. Those aren't alerts about when you're mentioned; those are alerts about when FEMA has something important you may want to know about.

There are a number of third-party apps that can monitor keywords and key phrases because Twitter doesn't support that capability. Of the different choices, we like Topsy (topsy.com),

Figure 7.5　Who's talking about Joel and what are they saying?

which offers a rich search language and even the ability to see trends and 30-day traffic for the word or phrase specified. Figure 7.6 shows an alert for "twitter power."

Use Topsy to monitor references to a specific Twitter account, for example, and you'll be able to check out who's part of the discussion and even reply to his or her tweets directly from the Topsy interface.

If you're familiar with Google Alerts (google.com/alerts), then you'll understand how Topsy works: it's a darn similar idea, just focused specifically on Twitter.

Set up filters in your e-mail client, and you'll soon have all of your keywords arranged into folders so that you can see which Twitter users are most interested in the topics your business covers.

For example, you could have one alert—and one folder—for tweets that mention your username. Another alert could cover mentions of your business's name. Another could look for mentions of your blog and another the title of your e-book, your main product or your topic, and so on.

Figure 7.6   Who's talking about "Twitter Power" right now? Topsy can help answer that, and send e-mail alerts to ensure we keep up on the conversation.

Don't forget to monitor your competitors on Twitter, too. Who's talking about them? What are they sharing? It's invaluable data!

Now you have to act on that data.

Obviously, the first thing you should do is to make sure that you're following those Twitter users. They're going to be tweeting about all sorts of other topics, too, but because these people are of interest to you, you'll want to know what they're saying.

This is exactly what Twitter is for.

You'll then want to start bringing them into your conversation.

If they haven't replied to one of your tweets already, then start by introducing yourself or, better, replying to one of their tweets and offering good information.

Even if they've mentioned only your subject rather than your name or one of your products, there's still a good chance that they'll know who you are, so it shouldn't be difficult to get them to respond and start building a relationship.

Once you have that relationship, you'll want to make the most of it. Before you release a new product, send a quick note to your top evangelists to ask for their opinion or feedback.

Give them sneak peeks of what you're doing so that they'll rush off and tell their friends.

If you see that they've left a great recommendation for you in a tweet, direct message them to give them a bonus reward.

When they mention that they bought your latest product or that they're reading your blog post, drop them a tweet to ask for their reaction and thoughts on the topic. They'll be thrilled, and you'll likely get a testimonial on their timeline.

When you can see who is saying nice things about you—and what they're saying—you can take all sorts of steps to encourage them and keep them spreading the word.

If they're saying good things, it's like having a constant stream of referrals and recommendations right on your profile page.

Your Personal Help Desk

Your evangelists and promoters are people who are going to be helping you anyway. They do that because they like you and your business. They're excited about it, they enjoy the benefits it brings, and they want their friends to share those benefits, too.

Only a small number of your followers are going to fit into this category, though. The rest are going to be people who are interested in your adventures, your opinions, and what you do and who want to know what you're doing right now.

Don't forget about them, however, because those people can still bring a huge amount of value to your business.

We've already seen how they can help you spot problems before you launch products. But they can also help you in all sorts of other ways. Because the site is filled with experts who possess all sorts of specialized knowledge, Twitter can also be a one-stop help desk for whatever you're struggling with, whether technical, business, or personal.

The easiest way to find help is simply to ask the people you know whether they can supply it. (See Figure 7.7.)

Obviously, this is going to work best when you have a bigger base of followers. The higher the number of people following your tweets, the greater the chances that one of them will be able to lend a hand.

That means that as you're building your followers, it's worth paying attention to what each of them does and considering the sort of help they might be able to offer in the future.

Choose to follow a Web design expert, for example, and you could then be reading some interesting tweets that could help spark your own design ideas. Better yet, if you can get the designer to sign up as one of your followers, then when you ask a question about Web design, there's a good chance that you'll get an answer direct from a professional.

It's also worth looking at the number of followers your followers have. If you can get followed by a few people with massive audiences, there's always a chance that your requests for help will be passed along or that their readers will click through to see your tweets.

Figure 7.7   Mystery writer A. L. Jambor puts out a call for help with Adobe Photoshop.

Followers with lots of followers of their own can provide outlets to plenty of help.

So how do you ask for that help?

You could certainly come straight out and ask whether anyone knows a skilled programmer or a great copywriter or where you can get a good logo designed.

That would be very simple, and depending on the size and makeup of your followers, there's a very good chance that it would give you results.

You could also ask your followers to retweet your message to help you find the assistance you need.

Again, every time you do this, you're spreading your name across the Twitterverse. People like to help and they like to show off their own expertise. So when someone tweets back with the information and advice you were looking for, you get to appear in his or her timeline, and he or she gets to look like an expert.

Everyone wins.

DON'T FORGET THE REAL WORLD

Twitter isn't necessarily the best place to find the help you need for your business, however. Both Dave and Joel believe that conferences can often be far more effective and valuable. In fact, we're both huge fans of conferences, workshops, seminars, and even local meet ups. They're fantastic places to learn new skills, become aware of outstanding opportunities, and meet other entrepreneurs keen on starting joint ventures and bursting with ideas.

In fact, we don't understand why people don't go to as many conferences as they can afford and can fit into their schedules.

One of the most effective bonus uses for Twitter is to follow tweets from people attending conferences, whether you're attending the event or not.

If you aren't at the conference, of course, it's never going to be as effective as being there in person, but it can still prove valuable.

If you know someone—or even better, a group of people—who is attending a conference, make sure that you're following his or her tweets. You should be able to pick up an idea of what people are saying, the sort of advice the speakers are offering, and the questions people are asking.

It might even be possible to tweet back with your own questions for someone at the conference to ask on your behalf.

We still encourage you to attend conferences and other professional events, but if there are some that you can't make, Twitter can help you get a taste of what you're missing—and tap a truly expert source.

Both of these approaches, though, are about you extracting help from your followers. That's valuable, but it works the other way, too.

Yes, you should be offering solutions whenever you see people asking questions in your field. We've already seen how that can be a great way to win followers and show off your own skills.

But it's even more important that you supply help that directly relates to your business.

This is where tracking keywords related to your business is so important.

WHAT IF THEY DON'T LIKE YOU?

It would be nice if every tweet that mentions the name of your business said what a great company you have, how awesome your products are, and that absolutely everyone should buy absolutely everything you're selling, then buy some more of your product or service for their families.

But life isn't like that.

Inevitably, you're going to see tweets from people who just weren't happy.

Some of them won't be happy with the quality of your product. They'll find that it didn't do what they hoped it would do—even if their expectations were way off base.

Others will complain about customer service. For some people, if their 2 AM query about a feature isn't answered within 10 minutes, the company hates them and should be penalized. For others, they might believe that a money-back guarantee lasts forever and that if they don't get a refund four years after buying your product, something's wrong with your company.

And others will have encountered a bug, a mistake, or an inaccuracy that they want to highlight.

Whatever the reason, whenever you see a complaint that relates to your product, jump on it.

Ask them what the problem is. Show that you're prepared to work with them to try to fix it. And when you do fix it, let them know by sending them a reply tweet so that everyone can see.

When you do that, you pick up a number of important benefits.

You stop that bad publicity in its tracks. If positive viral marketing can have fantastic effects on your sales, negative tweets can seriously restrict your growth.

You also get to turn a complainer into an unpaid member of your quality assurance team.

That old saying, "The customer is always right," might not always be right (sometimes the customer is just plain wrong, but it's right not to tell him or her), but you can always learn something from a customer complaint.

When soda company Spindrift saw a tweet from a convenience store clerk complaining about the staples on the boxes, its staff was quick to reply with a kind message and even an offer to send some free product to help ease the pain, so to speak (see Figure 7.8).

Because there's no limit to the number of Twitter accounts you can set up, you could create a separate account that functioned as an online, real-time help desk if user requests started to overwhelm your marketing-focused account.

Your customers would know where to come for help, and everyone would see that you're dedicated to meeting customers' demands.

Twitter is as much a conversation tool as a broadcasting device. Used carefully, you can have fantastic chats with your customers and your clients.

You can have conversations that help you spot problems before your product is released and win feedback and reviews.

You can follow conversations so that you can see what people are saying about you—and encourage them to keep on saying nice things about you.

Figure 7.8   Spindrift (@spindriftfresh) gets and responds promptly to customer feedback, even offering free product to the Twitterer.

And you can talk to those people who are less than completely happy, turning your Twitter account into the kind of open-access help desk that your customers will love and your potential customers will appreciate.

But you can also use Twitter to talk to your staff and your team. That's what we're going to discuss in the next chapter.

8

Leveraging Twitter for Team Communication

It's a conundrum. Twitter relies on tiny little posts and yet the effect is massive. It's certainly been massive for the people who created the site, but it's also huge for relationships between people. For both Joel and Dave, readers of their blogs and followers of their tweets can see what they're doing, where they're going, and what's interesting to them throughout the day. Instead of relying on an occasional blog post, they get brief updates that, because they take only a second to write, come in regularly.

Now we're not a distant friend who sends occasional letters. We're the guys in the next office they pass in the corridor.

That makes a huge difference to the way any online entrepreneur interacts with his or her customers but also is a big change for anyone else involved in his or her business.

Joel has a home office in Denver, Colorado, and employs freelancers scattered around the country and even around the world. It's one of the benefits of the digital age: he can hire the best people for the job wherever they may be. Dave doesn't even have an office: he works out of coffee shops and coworking spaces scattered throughout Boulder, Colorado, because he, too, has an extended staff.

Let's stick with Joel for now because some of those people have been working with him for years, and yet he's never met them. Joel can count on the fingers of half a hand the number of times he's spoken on the phone to some of them. Lots of other entrepreneurs do the same thing, and plenty of people today are competing with Dave for table space, considering their local coffee shop their prime working space.

These days you don't need to be in the same office as someone working on the same project to get the task done. As long as everyone has a reliable Internet connection, your team members can be thousands of miles apart.

Although telecommuting means you're not limited to your local labor pool, it does have its disadvantages. A team member you never see and never talk to can feel remote. The connection between you isn't the same as that between you and someone in the same building. A remote team member will feel left out of the loop, and he or she won't be up-to-date with the changes happening in your company.

That means the member will be less able to help with those changes, and there's always the risk that he or she will be left behind.

When you're all Twittering, though, it's much easier to keep track of what everyone is doing.

You can see what others are working on, the team members can see what you're up to, and you'll all feel much closer.

Twitter for Virtual Team Leaders

The best news is that those tweets don't even have to be work related. Although a tweet updating everyone on the team about the project the team is building will certainly be helpful, a quick note offering a prediction for the night's ball game or revealing what's in one's grocery bag can be useful, too.

That's because of Twitter's power as a digital watercooler.

It's a place where people come to hang out, shoot the breeze, and talk about things that aren't business oriented at all.

And just as those sorts of random conversations in person make people feel closer to each other, tossing out random thoughts on Twitter can have the same effect.

You could say what you're doing, add a link to a blog you're reading, or reply to someone else's tweet. The frequent reminders keep everyone in each other's minds, and *the thoughts themselves let everyone understand who the writer is.*

Twitter has been criticized because people share a lot of trivial, seemingly pointless information. One company even reported that 40 percent of all tweets are pointless babble. What nonsense. Most conversation is pointless babble, but it's that small talk that deepens trust, builds relationships, and allows people to like each other. Employees and team members don't just work for money. They also work for the satisfaction of the job they're doing. They stay with their current companies and continue working on their current projects because they find the challenge interesting—and because they *like* the people they're working with.

These connections are then as much a part of incentivizing workers as the more traditional bonuses and stock options are.

When your team is scattered and members never meet face-to-face, connections are very weak, and it becomes easy for a team member to drift away and be lured by another project with a different group.

This is the tip of a big change in business, too: loyalty can no longer be taken for granted even at the most established of brick-and-mortar companies, so it certainly can't be assumed at firms connected only by the Internet.

When team members feel that they're working with real people for a real person—people who play video games, teach their kids soccer, cook lasagna on the weekends, and so on—they become part of a community. And that makes it considerably harder to walk away. They're not betraying an e-mail; they're leaving a friend in the lurch. (See Figure 8.1.)

You're likely to be sending these kinds of personal, informal tweets anyway.

You're also likely to be sending out tweets that announce blog updates or that invite your followers to check out your new release. But don't limit yourself to those functional Twitter updates: nonbusiness tweets can have an even greater benefit for your business.

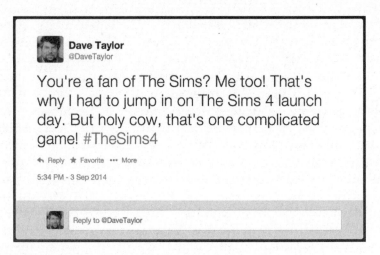

Figure 8.1   Now everyone knows Dave likes video games.

Creating a Twitter Account for a Virtual Team

Making sure that your Twitter timeline includes at least some informal tweets will help you connect with your virtual team. But it's not a strategy that's dedicated just for the virtual team because those team members form only a subset of your followers. As a result, they might even end up feeling a bit like interlopers, watching the conversation from the outside.

If that's a potential problem and you want to really get them involved, you can build a new online community by creating a dedicated Twitter account for the team.

There's no reason why a team leader can't create a Twitter account specifically for members of the team.

All team members will then feel that they're members of an exclusive club. They'll also know that they're building something as part of a team, rather than just flying solo. The greatest risk is that communication that should remain private will find its way into the public. Just as you can monitor the conversations of people who mention your products, so also your competitors can follow what you're saying to your team members—unless you keep your tweets private.

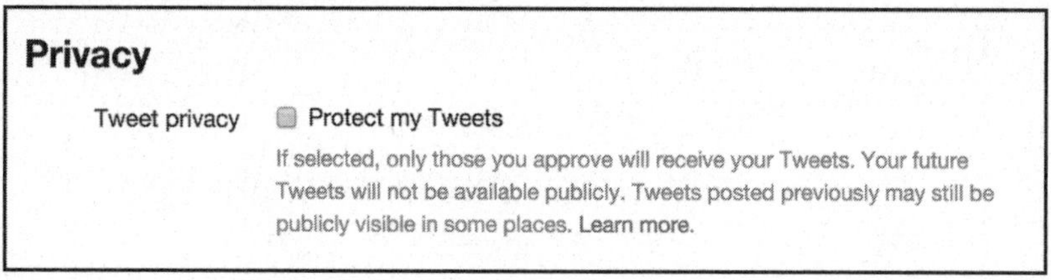

Privacy

Tweet privacy   ☐ Protect my Tweets

If selected, only those you approve will receive your Tweets. Your future
Tweets will not be available publicly. Tweets posted previously may still be
publicly visible in some places. Learn more.

Figure 8.2 Protect your updates and your team chats will stay
private.

Click the *Protect my Tweets* check button on the Settings page
of your Twitter account, and only the people you approve will be
able to follow your updates. (See Figure 8.2.)

You're not going to have many followers with this particular
privacy setting, and you're not going to be driving people to your
sites or blog. But that's not the point. You will have created an
online forum where your team members can talk, interact, and
keep everyone updated on the progress of the project without
prying eyes knowing what's going on.

There are some disadvantages here, though.

Not all of your team members are going to be familiar with
Twitter or feel comfortable writing in 140-character posts. You're
likely to find that this strategy works best with people who already
know how to use the system and do it anyway.

And although it works in real time, you want your team members to be working on the project, not spending their time writing
tweets! This, fortunately, can be accomplished simply by modeling
the behavior you expect, sharing an occasional off-topic tweet or
joke, but otherwise sticking to the business at hand.

Use a team Twitter account to troubleshoot problems, request
help, and provide updates, but try to keep the tweets as professional as possible.

Building a Team with Twitter

So, Twitter can help keep together an established team. It can do
that by helping scattered members understand that they're working alongside each other and that they're not alone. And it can do it

Figure 8.3   Developer Andy Matthews finds additional programmers for his company through Twitter.

by providing an online clubhouse where they can get together to keep everyone informed.

But the site can also be used to put those teams together in the first place.

When you need help with your business, there are all sorts of places you can look. We've had a lot of luck with Elance, a job site for freelancers, but word of mouth, personal websites, and even friends and family can all be good sources of team members. (See Figure 8.3.)

In fact, you're likely to be overwhelmed by options, which is not a good thing. Choosing the right person isn't easy, and you could find yourself wasting lots of time bringing new team members up to speed just to find that they need to be replaced.

Fortunately, with a bit of planning, Twitter can make these hiring decisions a great deal safer and easier.

The fact that someone is on Twitter is already a good sign. That shows that the person is not scared of new technology and that he or she is used to communicating and staying in touch at a distance—important considerations when you're building a virtual team.

But candidates' use of Twitter also reveals far more about them than you're likely to find on any resume or portfolio.

Of course, you'll want to read their resume and portfolio, check references, and so on, you know, the usual stuff associated with hiring. Designers, for example, should demonstrate their design skills on their Twitter page, on their resume, and in their portfolio. But there's more to working with someone than the quality of the work he or she delivers.

There's also the question of candidates' reliability, their professionalism, their ability to keep to deadlines, their communication skills, and whether they're pleasant people to work with.

When you anticipate working with someone over the long term, all of those elements are going to be important—and not all of them will be visible on his or her professional website.

Read candidates' tweets, however, and you'll be able to see not just what their work is like but also what they're like.

You can start with a search. Toss in a keyword that only a professional with the sort of skills you need is likely to use. If you were looking for a designer, for example, you could see who is using the term "responsive design." (See Figure 8.4.)

If you were hunting for someone to help with your website, you could see who's been tweeting about "Ruby on Rails" or simply "Ruby."

If you were looking for a copywriter to produce a sales page, you could search for terms such as "copy," "headline," or "call to action."

Clearly, not all of those people are going to be available for freelance work. But some will be, and you can add terms such as "freelance" or "contract" to narrow down the search.

Once you've managed to find a few freelancers with the skills you need, the fun can really begin. You'll be able to read their tweets to see how friendly they are and what they like to discuss.

There are a couple of things worth paying particular attention to as you go through this process, however.

First, note how often they answer questions.

Asking technical questions is nice—just knowing how to ask requires some knowledge—but more important is knowing how to answer. That demonstrates an even higher level of knowledge,

Figure 8.4 Don't know what these people are talking about; they must be designers.

and even more important, it also shows a willingness to help people—and that, after all, is why you're hiring someone.

But note, too, how candidates use jargon. Are they comfortable with the technical terms? Do they appear to be familiar with the latest technology?

And even more important, look at whom they're following and who's following them.

The true experts in a field are likely to have created their own communities of like-minded and similarly skilled professionals. They might not have done so deliberately, but if they're tweeting about their profession and providing good information, there's a great chance that other professionals will be following them.

If you don't want to approach that top professional—or if he or she is not available for hire, or you simply can't afford him or her—then following his or her own follow list could lead you to others in the field, too.

This strategy also works in reverse.

It's a very simple formula that requires little more than careful searching, a polite approach, and the understanding that you're not going to win a job with every follow.

Twitter works wonderfully when used by individuals to broadcast information about themselves and to keep in touch with other individuals across the Twitterverse.

It can also be hugely beneficial to businesses relying on scattered teams, allowing them to create the kind of bonds that previously could be formed only in offices.

But Twitter is also used to build brands.

9

Using Twitter to Help Build Your Brand

Online advertising has really spoiled everyone. Not only can advertisers now finely target where their ads appear, making sure that they're shown only to people most likely to find them interesting, but they also can track what happens after those ads go online.

They can measure how many people see the ads, how many click to learn more, and most important, how many purchase the advertised product as a direct result of seeing their ad.

With that kind of targeting and data, it's no wonder that Google, with its industry-leading AdWords ad network, is worth billions of dollars.

But the old advertising system didn't disappear. Drive down any highway and you're still going to see giant billboards drawing your eye and advertising businesses.

Times Square still has its neon lights, and neither Dish nor DirecTV have rid television programs of commercial breaks every 10 minutes.

The Internet might have changed some of the ways that advertising works, but brand building is still just as important as it used to be. In fact, we think it's considerably more important in the age of Twitter.

If you want people to know who you are and remember the name of your business, you have to keep putting it in front of them time and time again, and you also need to interact with them.

That's what traditional advertising has always aimed to do. An advertiser who bought a radio spot in the 1950s wasn't expecting to see a spike in sales immediately after the ad was broadcast. But the advertiser was expecting to see the product's name recognition increase. Customers would become familiar with the product, and over time, as they absorbed the advertising message, they'd trust the company and eventually buy the product.

On the Internet that's been done with banner ads that keep a product's name visible at the top of a Web page and with campaigns that pay for each thousand views rather than for each click that the ad receives.

And it can be done now with Twitter, too.

Twitter has proved a very valuable branding tool, and that hasn't been lost on big corporations. (See Figure 9.1.)

Figure 9.1   Southwest Airlines is just one company that uses Twitter to talk to customers and build a brand.

Just some of the companies you can find on Twitter include Carnival Cruise Line (@CarnivalCruise), Delta Air Lines (@Delta), JetBlue Airways (@JetBlue), Dell (@Direct2Dell), Amazon.com (@amazondeals), Forrester Research (@forrester), GM (@GM), and our favorite, M&M's (@mmsgreen and @mmsred).

All of these companies are using Twitter to build a loyal following with their customers and promote their brand. In this chapter, we'll explain some of the most important things to bear in mind when you endeavor to do the same thing for your business.

Create a Story

At its most basic, branding can simply mean putting the name of a product or a company where people can see it. That makes the name familiar so that a customer recognizes it on the shelf.

In practice, of course, branding does much more than that. It also attaches the product's name to a story so that when the customer sees the brand, he or she trusts it and associates the story with it.

That trust and attachment are keys to successful branding, and both start with a story.

Before you begin using Twitter to brand your company, then, you first need to think about what you want that brand to say. Do you want your product to look cool and streetwise or luxurious and exclusive? Do you want it be associated with ideas of health and nature, or would it sell better if customers considered it at the peak of technological development?

Look at how competing products sell themselves, and decide how you want your product to appear in the market. Usually, rather than trying to create a brand from scratch, you'll be able to create a variation on a general theme used in your industry.

Internet marketers, for example, might be a mixed bunch, but many of us like to appear in suits. That shows that although we might spend our days writing Web content and creating products, we're really traditional businesspeople who broker deals and negotiate partnerships. We'll then try to mark ourselves out within that niche with a brand that represents our unique personalities.

Joel uses a straightforward picture on his Twitter page, for example, and his bio describes him as an author and speaker, but also lists that he wears a size 10 shoe. That down-to-earth image might accurately reflect who Joel is, but it's also a part of his brand. People know when they read his blog or other writing that he's just a regular guy with a good business who's prepared to share what he's learned.

Yanik Silver, on the other hand, who is one of the world's leading Internet marketers, is much more of a daredevil. His bio includes the term *adventurer,* and his photo shows him hanging over a computer like Tom Cruise in *Mission Impossible.* That action stuff is part of his brand—and a part of his story. (See Figure 9.2.)

One product that does a very careful job of creating the right story for its market—and does it through Twitter—is M&M's. By giving different colored candies different personalities, Mars, the manufacturer, is able to appeal to different kinds of buyers. (See Figure 9.3.)

Figure 9.2 Leading Internet marketer Yanik Silver (@yaniksilver) creates an adventurous brand on Twitter.

Figure 9.3   M&M's uses two types of brand images on Twitter. Here you can see the popular green M&M's, but look closely for the red M&M's tweet in the figure, too. Two characters for two markets. Smart.

Twitter, therefore, has a timeline for green M&M's (@mmsgreen), which is targeted toward women, but it has another timeline "written" by the red M&M (@mmsred), which associates itself with car racing, basketball, and related sports to appeal more to men.

It's likely that you already have a good idea of the kind of story you want your brand to portray. So how can you use Twitter to put that story across?

Portraying Your Brand with Your Profile

We saw earlier in this book how the background of the profile can be a useful way of providing your followers with more information than you can squeeze into a bio.

By creating a sidebar on the left of the page, you can send followers to your other websites, where they might be able to do a range of different things, from clicking your ads to making purchases.

Those are direct results. When you're using Twitter to build a brand, though, you don't need your followers to type a uniform resource locator (URL) into their browser or make a purchase right away. You just want them to remember you.

That means producing a design that makes your brand memorable and that sums up you or your company.

Southwest Airlines, for example, used to use an image of its planes' tail as its photo and chose the sky as its background image. Today, it has a sidebar with links and testimonials, but it also includes a logo showing the plane surrounded by hearts to emphasize its image as the LUV airline. Either way, readers can see immediately whose page they're reading, and they understand what the company does.

The old M&M's Twitter page used the green candy to push the brand in the run-up to Valentine's Day. Mars matched the color scheme and graphics with the subject of the campaign.

Mars has gone a little further in its branding of M&M's. Not only did it create two pages, but it also changes its design so that the brand's image suits the current campaign. And then there's bacon. Yes, bacon. Even the M&M's team got into the act, as you can see in Figure 9.4.

It was certainly memorable, and the image alone was enough to help the page stand out.

But the profile doesn't have to be spectacular to convey the story of your brand, be instantly recognizable, and stick in the mind. For a long time, Whole Foods Market (@WholeFoods), for example, simply used a plain green background to match its green image and its logo as its picture. Today, it features simple foods on a plain tablecloth and a sidebar. (See Figure 9.5.)

That's very simple—and still very effective.

When you're using Twitter for branding, then, your background image is going to be important. You can choose an image that's complex and carefully designed—and change it as you change your marketing—or you can opt for something very simple but that still does the job.

More important is the style you use in your tweets.

Figure 9.4   According to M&M's, bacon was to be the newest flavor.
Sad news, though: it was just an April Fool's prank.

Figure 9.5   Whole Foods Market goes for simple, straightforward
foods and a plain logo for its Twitter branding.

Tweet Style—What to Say When You're Building a Brand and How to Say It

Jonathan Fields's response to being followed by an airline company minutes after tweeting about it wasn't completely positive. *Businessweek* quoted him as saying that he was "totally startled" and that, at first, he thought that JetBlue had noticed him because he was using the airport's wireless network.

The feeling was a mixture of respect for the company's diligence and use of technology—and general creepiness about the fact that it was watching him.

Clearly there is a danger for companies using Twitter to communicate with customers and build their brand. When they put themselves in the public arena, there's a chance that they can do more harm than good. Firms that get social media wrong look like interlopers, uninvited guests who have gate-crashed the cool people's party.

That doesn't just mean that they're missing all of the opportunities that the social media site offers. It can also show that the company just doesn't get it. That could have as negative an effect on its sales as good tweeting can have a positive effect.

A company needs to do a few things to blend in on Twitter and make sure that the image it's putting across on the site strikes a chord.

The first thing it needs to do is *be human*.

The company that really stands out for maintaining a personal touch on Twitter is telecommunications giant Comcast.

Comcast takes a huge amount of flack on Twitter. Twitterers are constantly complaining about the company's poor phone-based customer service. No one, though, seems to be complaining about its Twitter-based customer service at @comcastcares. The account is run by Will Osborne, the director of digital care for Comcast, who puts his own picture rather than the company logo on the bio. It also includes an e-mail address for people to write to and broadcasts tweets that look like they're coming from a Twitterer, not some company rep. (See Figure 9.6.)

Note how the company puts together a whole bunch of different strategies on the platform.

Figure 9.6 Comcast shows that it cares by giving its tweets a human face.

- ◆ It's chosen a name that doesn't just reflect the company but that also refutes a common criticism made of the corporation on Twitter.

- ◆ It's used a background image that highlights that a group of professionals is paying attention to you, the customer.

- ◆ Its tweets are written by a named individual who converses with the company's customers; it doesn't just broadcast messages to them.

- ◆ And @comcastcares follows a lot of people, demonstrating that it's listening as well as talking.

As we'll see, these characteristics appear in the timelines of many other successful companies on Twitter. They're also characteristics that are missing from companies that are really trying to make the most of Twitter—and failing.

Best Buy also used a real person rather than a logo to front its corporate Twitter page. Unlike Comcast, though, when Best Buy first started using Twitter, it made all sorts of mistakes that serve up a valuable lesson for any business thinking of using Twitter for branding.

First, the name was wrong. The company had registered *BestBuy* but was using it for a community-building project that had almost nothing to do with the main brand. It had no updates, was following no one, and had only a handful of followers. After presumably seeing other companies use Twitter far more effectively, @BestBuy is now a primary channel for the company, though a close examination of its follower:following ratio shows that it's mostly a broadcast channel, not a way to engage with its customers. See Figure 9.7 to see what we mean.

Although Osborne looks happy, friendly, and approachable in his image, the sales team in Best Buy's image look like actors paid to be peppy sales staff. And why don't they have a store full of happy customers and cool electronics behind them anyway?

Figure 9.7   Best Buy still has a ways to go to get the most out of its Twitter account.

The overall impression isn't that this is a friendly, helpful company that wants to improve its customers' experience but that this is a company that just wants to sell product.

A close examination of the Best Buy page reveals that it also has @BestBuySupport, which is a step in the right direction, but an examination of that particular timeline shows that it might be too personal, with its 5,100 followers, one person it follows, and seven posts in 30 days (see Figure 9.8).

Having a human—rather than a corporate—presence on Twitter might involve actually showing a human face in the way that Comcast does. But it will always involve tweeting in *an informal, friendly manner.*

Twitter, after all, is a very personal place. It's a site that asks a personal question and lets people share their random thoughts with the world at large.

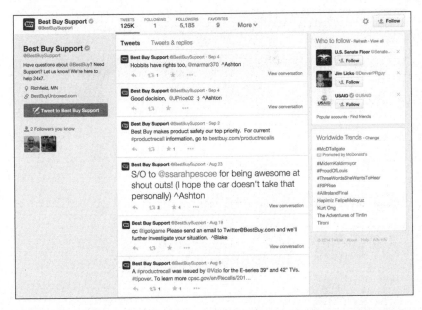

Figure 9.8   Best Buy does have a customer support account, but is it using it to best advantage with just a few thousand followers and only one tweet every four to five days?

Businesses that tweet like a corporate executive addressing a board meeting will stand out on the site and scream that they have no idea what they're doing—or whom they're talking to.

Starbucks, for example, has a number of timelines, but its main Twitter presence, @Starbucks, consists mostly of a customer representative answering questions. The company appears to be using the site as an extension of its customer service—one very simple corporate use for Twitter. It uses a logo instead of a personal image, but Archana, Jeremy, and Madeline, the employees responsible for managing the account, aren't afraid to talk about their personal experiences. (See Figure 9.9.)

Although it's clear that this is a corporate Twitter account, because the tweets are written in such a friendly, laid-back manner, Starbucks does create the impression that the followers are chatting with the barista in exactly the way they might do at the café itself—and that the café itself is a friendly, relaxed place to be.

Figure 9.9 Starbucks shows that it's a relaxed place to hang out with friendly, easygoing tweets.

That's good branding.

So, your tweets should be friendly. They have to sound like they're coming from a real person, from another member of the Twitter community, and not from some creepy company that's listening for a mention of its name. (See Figure 9.10.)

But what should those tweets say to build a brand image that's positive and memorable?

In practice, corporate tweets that try to build brands tend to fall into four broad categories:

1. Company news

2. Customer support

3. Feedback

4. Special offers

Figure 9.10   Delta Air Lines (@Delta) disappeared for a while but then woke up. Now it likes to share customer photos, as shown.

NEWS

We've already seen that posting only news updates on Twitter can make for an ineffective timeline. But including some carefully chosen news posts can have a positive branding effect. They reward the follower with useful information, and they show that the company is enthusiastic about what it's doing.

That enthusiasm can be infectious.

Clearly, you have to be careful to make sure that you're broadcasting the right kind of news and that you're doing it in the right way.

Usually one of the most important rules for releasing news about a company is whether it passes the *Who cares?* test. (See Figure 9.11.)

In general, no one cares what companies are up to. If your local medical clinic had just repainted its waiting room, why would you care?

You wouldn't care unless that information actually affected you. If the clinic had changed its phone number or fired your doctor, then you'd want to know.

Dave Taylor
@DaveTaylor

Heading into the @9NEWS studios tomorrow afternoon to talk about the iPhone 6. Sadly, I won't have one in hand. But look for me on TV!

↩ Reply ★ Favorite ••• More

9:26 AM - 7 Sep 2014

Figure 9.11   Dave's heading into the local TV news channel studio to talk about technology. Who cares? Well, he does and by showing that he's excited about it, his fans will get excited, too—and feel that if his local TV channel considers him an expert, then they should follow him as well.

If it had changed its design, you probably wouldn't want to know.

On Twitter, that rule still holds to some degree: news announcements that affect the reader are always going to be the most interesting. But even an announcement that a company has changed its blog design or squished another bug in its application can be interesting if it looks like gossipy fun.

The best way to handle news for branding, then, is to mix it in with other kinds of content and to add a personal comment so that it sounds like it's coming from a real person and not from a company.

CUSTOMER SUPPORT

Customer support on Twitter is often seen by companies as the only reason to use the service. Once they have someone Twittering away and answering questions, they feel that they've done their job and that there's nothing else to do.

That's a big mistake.

It's not just a mistake because doing it badly—like Best Buy originally did and still to some extent does—can actually put people off. It's also a mistake because good customer service is powerful branding.

It shows that the company is available to anyone who needs its help and that it listens, too, and in an era where most of us are used to being ignored by the companies we purchase from, it's a big differentiator.

The Home Depot (@HomeDepot) does this very, very well. Its tweets offer short, seasonal tips to keep people reading, but its real strength is the quality of its customer support. Even though one Twitter account can address only a fraction of the questions the company's customers are going to have, the impression it creates is that followers will find even better help at the store itself. (See Figure 9.12.)

That's exactly what branding should do: make potential customers feel that the real thing is even better.

Include great customer service tweets in your timeline—tweets that address problems and tell people exactly where they can find

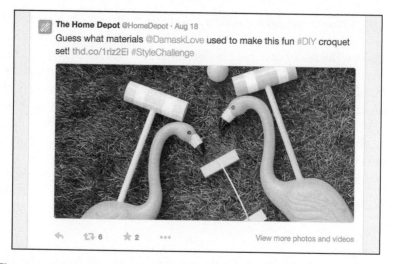

The Home Depot @HomeDepot · Aug 18
Guess what materials @DamaskLove used to make this fun #DIY croquet set! thd.co/1riz2Ei #StyleChallenge

6   2   ...   View more photos and videos

Figure 9.12   Home Depot reposts customer photos that are engaging, fun, and consistent with its do-it-yourself theme.

solutions—and you'll add one important characteristic to your branding story.

FEEDBACK

Feedback tweets are similar to customer service tweets but with an important difference. Customer service tweets are likely to be initiated by the customer. Instead of sitting on a phone line for half an hour, wondering whether they should press 1, push the hash key, or hurl the phone at the wall, customers can send a quick direct message to a company rep on Twitter and receive a response.

Ideally, the customer gets the answer he or she needs almost right away. The company gets to help one customer and show lots of other customers that it's helpful, friendly, and keen to lend a hand.

But not all customer service comments are sent as direct messages or even as replies to tweets on the company's own timeline. Often they're just comments—usually rants—on its own timeline.

A company looking to use Twitter for branding can spot those tweets through alerts and react to them in the hope that it can stop negative publicity from spreading.

That's not always possible, but again, it does show that the company cares and that even if it's not perfect, it is trying to improve. That can be an important part of a brand image, too.

Feedback, though, isn't just about listening to what people are saying about your company. It can also mean inviting people to say something about your company.

Starbucks has a second Twitter account at @MyStarbucksIdea that supports its My Starbucks Idea website (mystarbucksidea.force.com). The site lets customers send in their proposals to improve the company and see how they're implemented. (See Figure 9.13.)

The Twitter timeline allows the company to thank the customers for their ideas and explain what's happening to them.

It's a great way for the company to show that it sees itself as just one part of the Starbucks community—even if it doesn't produce immediate direct sales.

Figure 9.13 My Starbucks Idea gives customers feedback and shows that the coffee chain is listening.

Special Offers

Special offers are standard marketing practice, and as we've seen, they can work on Twitter as much as anywhere else. Reward followers for reading your tweets by giving them exclusive deals that they feel they can't get anywhere else, and you'll give them an incentive to keep reading. (See Figure 9.14.)

You'll also give yourself some extra sales.

Even an online publisher could do this by mentioning a great deal one of its affiliates is offering. Include either your affiliate link in the code or a link back to your Web page, and you might just generate some nice commissions.

Companies using Twitter for branding, though, have to be a little careful with the way they use special offers.

Although discounts can be a very powerful way to drive customers to take immediate action, branding doesn't demand action. It simply requires the follower to keep reading and to think about the company in a certain way.

Make lots of special offers and instead of thinking about the company as a trusted friend that always delivers quality goods and services, he or she will see it as a corporation keen to push its products.

Those special offers start to look like a hard sell, and hard selling doesn't work on Twitter or any other social media channel.

If you want to make immediate direct sales through Twitter, then regular special offers could be very effective. If you want to

Figure 9.14   Carnival Cruise Line (@CarnivalCruise) uses a range of social media strategies to promote its business and was a Twitter early adopter. It also shares special offers on its timeline.

use the site to build a brand and create a community around your firm, then special offers should be scattered throughout your timeline just to reward your followers and keep them interested.

There's no golden rule about how many promotions is too many. It all depends on what else you're saying and who's following you. If you're making offers more frequently than one in five tweets, though, then you're probably doing it too often.

Reinforce the Core Message

All of these tweets we've discussed should look familiar. There's a good chance that you're writing them anyway as you use Twitter to drive customers to take action.

But there's one type of tweet we haven't mentioned.

It's the one that the site was really created for and one that both Joel and Dave use frequently on their timelines: random thoughts.

People write all sorts of strange things on Twitter. It's one of the service's attractions. It's as though people have put a window on the side of their head and are letting the rest of us peek in every now and then to see what thoughts are passing through. (See Figure 9.15.)

Yes, it's a bit judgmental, and it really shouldn't be very interesting to anyone who isn't in the room with Joel.

But it really is!

Figure 9.15   One of Joel's random thoughts. They help with his brand image but would they help a company? We doubt it.

Tweets like these might be fun but they aren't actionable. Tell your followers that one of your affiliates is running a special offer and include the link to your site, and you can expect people to click through.

Break news about a blog post that you've just put up, and you can expect people to come and read it.

Write a tweet that tells people that you're thinking of eating a donut and to blazes with the calories, and the best you can hope is that they'll smile—and feel closer to you.

That's the benefit of these sorts of tweets: they create a better relationship with your followers, your customers, and your community.

By personalizing your Twitter stream, you're not just the owner of a website or some anonymous blogger on the Internet a million miles away. You're a real human being who thinks, works, suffers through overly perfumed people, and feels guilty about eating donuts.

That sort of feeling can do wonders for the connection you have with your customers and with your readers.

But do they help a company with its branding efforts?

A company's tweets should appear human, but unless the company brand is the person behind the company, the message isn't about the user; it's about the company itself. Adding what the Twitterer thinks about a piece of news he or she is broadcasting or about an answer to a customer's question shows that the company really does care. Mention that a corporation is in the mood for a hot fudge sundae, and it starts to look a little strange.

That isn't to say that random thoughts can play no part in branding on Twitter.

They do play a role *but only in personal branding.*

We use them in our timelines because they help brand us as regular guys. Well, mostly regular guys, at least! That brand is important because we don't want other entrepreneurs to feel that online marketing is only for people with tons of experience, who know how to program, or who understand everything there is to know about the Internet. The fact that anyone—even family-focused, game-playing, donut-eating guys like us—can do it is an important part of the story we want to put across.

The same may be true when the Twitterer embodies the core values of the company and is part of the corporate brand. Tony Hsieh, for example, is the chief executive officer (CEO) of Zappos, an online retail store. He tweets both as an individual and on behalf of his company at @tonyhsieh. Because this is his personal Twitter timeline, there's nothing wrong with Hsieh including random thoughts in his tweets—his tweets are first about him, not his company. (See Figure 9.16.)

But because he's also the CEO of Zappos, something his background image makes clear, what he says also reflects the company.

This isn't exactly the same as branding, though. Hsieh's tweets provide publicity for his company and build a community out of his customers. But beyond indicating that his company is open and approachable, they say little else about the firm.

Figure 9.16 Tony Hsieh, CEO of Zappos, builds a personal brand and promotes his company at the same time.

By personalizing his tweets in this way, Tony turns his time-line into a branding tool that reinforces his image as the CEO of Zappos.

British tycoon Richard Branson (@richardbranson) has made a fortune by portraying himself as the face of Virgin. His bio on Twitter: "Tie-loathing adventurer and thrill seeker, who believes in turning ideas into reality. Otherwise known as Dr Yes at @virgin!" He's become a celebrity, and every time he appears in the press, he's promoting his various businesses.

This is all about sticking to the core message. Once you know what you want your brand to look like and what you want it to say, it's important to make sure that your tweets say only that and don't confuse the message.

If you're tweeting on behalf of a company, keep it human but not too personal.

If you're tweeting on behalf of a personal brand, include the random thoughts but reduce the offers.

Those simple guidelines should help keep your tweets on message.

Repetition, Repetition, Repetition

To keep your tweets on message, though, you will also have to repeat them.

One of the challenges of any branding campaign is that the effect is never long lasting. That's why even companies such as Coca-Cola have to keep spending billions of dollars every year to keep their products in the public eye.

Fortunately, when you're using Twitter for branding, you don't have to spend billions, or even millions, of dollars to keep your market's attention.

You just have to keep sending out tweets.

There are companies that make the mistake of starting a Twitter campaign to promote a particular product, drop Twitter when the campaign ends, and then try to pick Twitter up again months later. This strategy can work—if you're not sending out tweets, you're not bothering anyone, so few followers will block your tweets. But you will lose momentum and your community can disappear.

In fact, this is why you'll hear both Dave and Joel, along with a lot of other social media marketing folk, talk about *engagement* being the secret of success. It's not enough just to broadcast your sales pitch occasionally, or even every day. You have to engage, to converse, and to participate in your market and chat with your customers.

When you're using Twitter as a branding tool, you need to be tweeting at least once a day, and ideally far more often than that, whether those messages are always on topic or not.

That doesn't have to be as hard as it sounds.

Writing the Tweets

I admit, it does sound hard. We like tweeting. It's fun, it's interesting, it's enjoyable, and the feedback and responses can be hilarious, poignant, and provocative. Joel and Dave have both had great virtual conversations with wonderful people from around the world, learned all sorts of fascinating things, and picked up information that we couldn't have learned any other way.

But it takes time, and when you're a busy executive using Twitter to promote your business rather than just tell the world what you had for breakfast, that time is an investment.

This is where the difference between a corporate Twitter account and a private Twitter account is important.

Zappos' CEO might be writing his own tweets, but not everyone does that. The tweets of big companies, such as Delta and Carnival Cruise Line, aren't written by the CEO. They're written by employees or public relations firms who have been given the job of promoting the company's brand on the Web.

You can do the same thing.

If you don't want to write your tweets yourself, hand over the job of creating your business's tweets to someone in your office. Let him or her be your company's Twitter—and social media!—presence. Give that employee the freedom to be human and include his or her opinions (as long as they're in alignment with your own) as well as your company's. You can even consider putting his or her name in the bio so that readers know who's behind the tweets.

You'll still get the familiarity with your followers that only Twitter can bring. But you'll do it without any effort, and your helper will likely enjoy the interaction and notoriety it brings, too.

Win Retweets

The best people to write your tweets for you are other Twitter users. When it comes to viral marketing and the ability to spread a brand message, nothing beats posting a tweet that flies around the Twitterverse. Instead of just showing your name to your followers, people who already know you, you get to be seen by their followers, by those followers' followers, and so on.

Being retweeted is like hitting the marketing jackpot.

But it's a jackpot that you can rig. With a little care, you can increase the chances that a tweet you post will be shared across Twitter.

Clearly, the more followers you have, the greater the chances that some of those followers will want to share your posts. But there's a lot more to winning retweets than just building a big follower list. According to Dan Zarrella (@danzarrella), a social media scientist who has conducted in-depth analyses of the way retweeted posts spread on Twitter, some types of tweets are more likely to be shared than others.

Content that's timely, such as news items, tend to be shared often, as do tweets about Twitter itself. Around 70 percent of retweeted posts contain links, says Zarrella, with list posts particularly popular. The most popular subjects to win retweets are news, instructional content, entertainment, opinion, products, and small talk, in that order.

Of course, links to giveaways also do well. To celebrate the thirtieth anniversary of the AAdvantage frequent-flier program, American Airlines ran a Twitter contest called "Tweet to Win 30K Miles." Participants had to register their AAdvantage account number on a custom microsite and send out a tweet with the "#Deal30" hashtag. Easy enough.

In the first week the site had 18,000 visitors, and the @AAdvantage Twitter account had a 70 percent increase in followers. By the time the campaign ended, AAdvantage retweets had increased almost 50 percent, and more than 27,000 AAdvantage members registered on the site for the promotion.

Give away valuable items or post links to exclusive, timely information related to your industry, and there's a very good chance that people will pass it on—especially if you're polite or witty. One of the most reassuring aspects of Zarrella's research is that the most popular words in retweeted posts are *you, twitter, please,* and *retweet.* Asking politely for a retweet really does work.

And the best news of all is that the click-throughs work, too. Zarrella's day job is with HubSpot, a company that sells inbound marketing software. Leads that reach HubSpot through Twitter, Zarella says, are among the prospects most likely to buy.

Create Hashtags and Run Hashtag Chats

Retweets help spread your brand. But if you also want to deepen your brand, show that you are knowledgeable about your industry, and demonstrate that your company is the leading source of information about your topic on Twitter, then hashtags can be particularly helpful.

A hashtag is simply a keyword marked with a # symbol. You've already seen them show up many times in this book! #ForReal.

By placing hashtags in tweets that cover a particular topic, people interested in following discussions about that subject on Twitter can easily find all the posts regardless of whether they follow all the people participating in the discussion.

That's particularly useful for breaking news stories. When wildfires threatened the California town of Santa Barbara, for example, residents were able to keep up-to-date with evacuation warnings by reading tweets with the hashtag #jesusitafire. After the Iranian elections in 2009, demonstrators let the world know what was happening by adding #iranelection to their tweets. More recently, #teaparty denoted discussion related to the conservative U.S. political group known as the Tea Party, and when hundreds of schoolgirls were kidnapped by rebels in northern

Nigeria in early 2014, the hashtag #BringBackOurGirls electrified world discussion.

On the local front, Dave kept track of the disastrous 2013 floods in his home town of Boulder, Colorado, by watching the #BoulderFlood hashtag on Twitter, staying up to the minute with breaking news.

On applications such as Tweetdeck, on which tweets are updated automatically, users were able to see an ongoing stream of news updates, staying in touch with events as they unfolded.

Most hashtags don't work in this way, though. Instead, they usually act as a kind of label allowing people to find a particular type of content. Aspiring novelists, for example, can search for #pubtips to read tips posted by literary agents about writing queries and getting published. Any agent who wants to share a tip only has to add the hashtag to a tweet to get his or her name in front of thousands of wannabe authors. It's a great way to become part of a community on Twitter, and contributing regularly to your industry's hashtags allows you to demonstrate your expertise to a select audience.

And if there aren't any active hashtags for your industry, there's nothing wrong with creating one. Simply tell your followers that you're creating a hashtag for a particular theme, and start adding it to tweets on that subject. So, the owner of a garden center, for example, could create a hashtag for gardening advice. Contribute plenty of tips and that business owner will come to be seen as a leader on his subject.

Hashtags really become powerful, though, when they're updated at set times in a kind of public, real-time chat session called a TweetChat. In addition to reading the #pubtips hashtag, for example, authors of children's books can also take part in #kidlitchat. Agents representing authors of children's books make themselves available to answer questions from writers and talk about the publishing industry. It's not as touchy-feely as a conference, but it does allow writers and agents to get together, trade information, and get to know each other.

Some chats are very organized. In fact, there are calendars of TweetChats, such as the one at http://blog.tweetchat.com/calendar/—as shown in Figure 9.17.

Figure 9.17   Tweetchat.com has a calendar with some of the many regular TweetChats that now happen on Twitter each week.

Recently, Dave was the guest on a TweetChat sponsored by credit-scoring company Experian: at a set time, he connected to Twitter, and every message he sent included the hashtag #MarketingChat, marking it as part of the discussion. Before that time, he'd sent a set of specific questions to the host that were then sent out every 5–10 minutes to keep the conversation lively. It was a fun and fast-paced hour of discussion and great branding for both Dave and Experian. Other chats, though, happen spontaneously. A group of experts who happen to be on Twitter at the same time sometimes decide to take questions for the next hour or so and invite people who want to take part to add a hashtag to the end of their tweets. Those are likely to bring in fewer people, but they can be fun and engage other Twitter users who also happen to be online.

Most important of all, though, when you're among the people answering questions, you position your brand as a leader that's reliable, knowledgeable, trustworthy, and willing to give back to the community. That's powerful branding.

Like any effective marketing channel, Twitter can be a valuable branding tool. It can work as a personal branding tool, giving any individual an image that's memorable and recognizable, and it can function as a corporate branding tool helping companies stand out, win trust, and turn their customers into a community.

Even some of the world's biggest companies have recognized the power of Twitter to drive home their message, and although not all of them are doing it correctly, a number have come up with some valuable models that anyone can copy.

Branding brings long-term results. You can also use Twitter to create instant results. In the next chapter, we're going to discuss some of the ways that you can drive behavior in your followers.

10

Leveraging Twitter to Drive Follower Behavior

We've seen that there are all sorts of different ways of writing tweets. We've seen that there are all sorts of different ways you can use Twitter, too.

The most common way marketers want to use Twitter, though, is to produce immediate results. They see their followers as a pool of people who will one day give them money—either directly or with the help of advertising—and they want to write tweets that create that effect.

There's nothing wrong with that. It's possibly a little short-sighted, but there's really nothing wrong with it.

You can certainly create tweets that drive your followers to take the steps that you want them to take. Sometimes. But you have to be careful.

Your Twitter timeline is not a sales page. Gripping headlines and hard calls to action on Twitter are more likely to drive people away than drive them to buy. Your tweets need to be subtle. You have to build interest and trust in your online community. Only then will your followers feel that doing what you want them to do will be worth their while.

In this chapter, which we think is the most important chapter in the book, we're going to explain how to drive traffic to a website, how to use surveys to gain data and build responses, and how to mine your customers for valuable feedback.

We'll then discuss how to build effective, action-oriented Twitter strategies and how to keep track of the results.

Let's start by looking at the ways that you can drive followers to a website.

Driving Followers to a Website

We've already seen that it's possible on Twitter to include a uniform resource locator (URL) in tweets. We've also seen that there are even systems available that can create these kinds of tweets automatically.

But that doesn't mean that anyone will click those links. Nor is this ability particularly useful if you want to send your followers to a site that isn't a blog.

Although driving traffic toward other content pages has to be one of the most common uses of Twitter, you might also want to send followers to a purchase page, to a registration page, or to a page on which you hope they'll click an ad.

All of these are possible on Twitter.

Promoting a Blog on Twitter

When people first started creating weblogs (*blogs* for short), they were nothing more than online diaries, a place for people to share their thoughts and feelings and let anyone else read them and add additional thoughts and comments.

Since the dawn of blogs, however, they've become so much more than that.

Today, blogs are a very effective publishing system. For most users, they've evolved to become sophisticated online magazines rather than old-school online journals or personal sites.

The benefit is that publishers can now write about anything they want—and get paid for it.

The disadvantage is that blogs are no longer personal.

If readers used to come to blogs to find out what the writer was doing or thinking, today's blogs are often not even written by the bloggers themselves. Good professional blogs tend to be filled with guest posts, paid writers, and ghostwriters. And there's nothing wrong with that.

The first thing that Twitter can do for a blog is bring back the personality of the writer.

Bloggers can use Twitter to give readers a peek behind the scenes of their business, provide quick notices about their plans and the posts they're working on, and answer direct questions put to them by readers.

Sure, you can also do all of this on your blog—and ideally, you should. (See Figure 10.1.)

When your blog really becomes popular, it's unlikely that you'll have time to respond to every comment your posts receive. Articles about your blog are also likely to be less interesting to your readers than posts about cars, photography, or whatever it is that users are visiting your site to see.

It's kind of like those *Making Of* videos included on the DVDs you buy: How many people actually watch them versus the number of people who enjoy the movie and are done?

Twitter can give publishers of blogs an alternative space to get closer to their readers, even when they're using content written by professional writers.

But what if you want to bring in new readers or increase the number of occasional visitors?

Twitter can help there, too.

Figure 10.1   Headline and blog post URL make for an easy tweet and some helpful extra traffic. But is a headline enough to turn a follower into a reader?

The principle is very simple. If you were to put an ad on Google AdWords to promote every blog post you publish, you'd have to pay a lot of money. Assuming you got the calculation right by comparing the cost of the ads against the revenue from any resultant ad clicks or product sales, you might make a small profit. But you'd need a lot of visitors to make it worthwhile.

Take that same announcement and tweet it, however, and the economics change: placing an announcement of a new blog post on Twitter is easy and lets lots of people know about it.

We've seen how Darren Rowse does this with his photography site, Digital Photography School—a fantastic example of a highly successful blog that's much more of a magazine than a personal diary.

That's one very simple way to drive traffic from Twitter to a blog.

But that works because Rowse's site is already well-known. He doesn't have to do anything but remind his regular readers that a new post is online for those readers to stop by and look at.

Rowse's personal timeline is much more complex. His tweets contain a mixture of news announcements about his blogs as well as personal comments and answers to readers' questions.

That combination is important. Blog post headlines by themselves look very weak on Twitter. Even the sort of hard-hitting headline that social media types love (something like "20 Ways to Gain More Followers") can look desperate when it appears in a tweet.

Instead of saying something *about* you, they tell readers that you really want them to be doing something *for* you: you want them to be reading your blog post.

That's exactly the wrong way to go about Twitter, and it's certainly the wrong way to go about driving followers to a blog post and making them regular readers.

Twitter works best by creating curiosity. People read your tweets, become a part of your life, and want to see what you're up to next. When you announce that you've just written a new blog post, they'll stop by to read it not just because the content is interesting but also because they're interested in what you wrote, or in what you published if you didn't write it yourself.

Curiosity doesn't come because of one tweet, however. It happens through regularly publishing good tweets.

When you first join Twitter, don't rush to fill your timeline with links that lead to your blog. Tweet about yourself, about what you are doing, are thinking, and would like to be doing.

Reply to what other people tweet, especially those people who appear to have an interest in your topic and in particular Twitter users with large followings, so that their subsequent reply to you will turn up in their timeline for everyone else to see.

Offer advice and solutions to Twitterers who have posed questions or are struggling with something in your field of expertise.

All of that will start to give you a core group of followers who are interested in who you are and what you can do for them. And so far, all you've done is help them. In effect, you will have been priming your market by handing out freebies in the form of free advice—a time-tested marketing strategy.

Now when you write about your latest blog posts, you should find that many of your followers will click through to read them. They'll know that you deliver good advice, and they'll be hungry for more.

You can then continue this strategy of providing regular updates of informative and entertaining tweets interspersed with links to your blog, online store, or even affiliate pages.

And if you've already started Twittering, then it's never too late to begin this strategy!

Just make sure that you've added plenty of interesting and useful tweets before you next post a link to your website.

Priming your followers in this way should help maximize your click-throughs, but let's keep in mind that blogs, like Twitter, are also generally a means to an end, not an end unto themselves: most publishers want their readers to click on an ad or make a purchase on the site.

With a little thought, you can use Twitter to increase the chances that will happen, too.

This takes a little skill and some planning. You have to know what type of ads are likely to appear on your website's pages, and you have to prepare your followers for them on Twitter.

If you're running Google AdSense, however, recognize that this strategy is going to be particularly difficult. We're both big fans of AdSense, and you should definitely be using it on your website—google.com/adsense—but because the ads change so unexpectedly, you can't tease interest in a particular product so that your readers are more likely to click on its ad. You can only create top-quality content and optimize the units so that readers click the ads to find out more.

Curiosity is a powerful driving factor on blogs, too.

But AdSense isn't the only way you can put ads on a blog, and therefore it's not the only way you can monetize your Twitter followers if you're not focused on product or service sales.

For example, perhaps you're running some cost per thousand ad campaigns that pay for every view you receive. Every person from Twitter who clicks through to your site will therefore generate additional revenue, even if the individual amounts are small.

More important is that you load up on affiliate ads. These are predictable—you choose the products—and unlike the products promoted in AdSense units, you can recommend these yourself.

Do you see how this creates a golden opportunity on Twitter?

Imagine that you ran a blog about video games. You could create a series of tweets about the latest game everyone's talking about.

The first tweet could say that you're going to buy it.

The second tweet could say that the graphics have blown you away and that it looks like a killer game.

The third tweet could say that you've discovered a bunch of fantastic strategies and that the game is even better than you expected.

And the fourth tweet would include the URL of a blog post that offered a complete review of the game or tips to complete it. Included on the Web page would be an affiliate ad from Amazon .com that led directly to the game.

You can add these affiliate links very easily by signing up as an Amazon Associate (the site's term for affiliates). You'll be able to choose the product you want to promote and paste the code onto your Web page. Every time someone clicks on that ad, you get a share of the revenue. (Just be sure to embed the link into your text. Most professional bloggers find that that's the best way to earn through Amazon.com's affiliate program.)

You'd need to run a tweet series like this quickly. You want people to buy from your site; you don't want them to get excited and buy directly from Amazon.com, cutting you out of the loop. To keep your keenest followers waiting for you—and for everyone else to catch up—you could tease that you're working on a must-read review. That should give them a reason to put off their decision to buy until they've read what you have to say—and seen your ad.

The result should be that Twitter gives you the chance to create a kind of teaser campaign that can give you affiliate earnings when you launch your blog post.

Twitter as a Resource for Post Ideas

With the right combination of tweets, you can use Twitter to drive followers to a page with a targeted ad. But you can also use your followers for another purpose, one that's just as valuable.

You can use them as a resource for blog post ideas.

Ask your followers what sort of posts they'd like to see on your blog, and you're likely to get swamped with ideas.

That makes life very easy for you.

At the beginning of every month, you could just ask your followers what issues they'd like to see covered on your blog in the next few weeks.

No more beating your head against the wall, trying to think up new content. No more wondering whether people are going to like the concept, either.

Before you write about a particular subject, you could just ask your followers what they think. If everyone says it sounds a bit dull or asks how you're going to deal with this aspect or approach to that problem you haven't even considered, you can start thinking again.

You won't have to wait until you've been sweating over the post for a couple of hours to discover it isn't going to work or that your approach has some inherent flaws you hadn't considered.

And, of course, once you've written it, you can be sure that when you announce that it's online, you'll have an audience for it. This can be fascinating stuff. Mine your followers for information and you'll be amazed at the responses you get. More important, asking a crowd for ideas will help keep your blog fresh and lively, an important consideration when you've been doing it for a while and you feel like you've already covered everything important in your topic area.

Indeed, we suggest that fatigue is one of the biggest dangers for a mature blog, but by having a giant bank of editorial advisors to call on, Twitter can help your blog stay fresh and engaging.

There are a couple of ways you can mine this kind of information.

The first is to ask a straightforward, open-ended question. A tweet that says, "What would you like to see covered on the blog this month?" could get you a ton of interesting answers.

A tweet that said, "Want to guest post on my blog? Send me a direct message" would land you a ton of interesting content.

Caveat: you do have to be careful with guest posts. Your blog is successful because *you* create it. You came up with the subject, you set the topics for the posts, and for the most part, you're likely to be writing it. Hand over too much influence to your readers—or followers—and there's a risk that you'll dilute the characteristics that have made your site so interesting.

Dave would say that it's letting the inmates run the asylum, but we're not going to characterize your followers and readers as lunatics. Well, mostly not!

It's also the case that although readers might say they want posts about this subject or content about that topic, they're often the worst judges of what they really need, and they certainly still need to be surprised by excellent content that they hadn't thought of themselves.

That's why a good alternative option is to give your followers a choice. Instead of asking them what content they'd like to see, offer them three subjects, and ask which they'd like to see most. That will give you a good idea of your followers' preferences, and if you get a close vote, you can still write about all of them.

Announcing your new blog posts on Twitter can help create more views and win you some extra revenue. Using your followers as a resource for post ideas can help keep your blog focused and informative. And, of course, the people who see tweets about your blog posts won't be restricted to your followers. Although your followers are likely to give you the highest number of click-throughs, plenty of people will also click through your timeline without following you. They'll see your blog links and your supporting tweets, and many of them will visit your blog as a result.

Those extra clicks, both from dedicated followers interested in you and your topic and from curious passers-by, are important reasons for marketing a blog on Twitter. It's why blog promotion is one of the main uses of Twitter, even if that use is often restricted to automated Twitter feeds.

But Twitter can do a lot more than drive followers to a blog page.

It can also drive them to buy.

Driving Followers to the Mall

Look through our timelines and you'll see lots of different kinds of tweets. You'll see links to blog posts. Photos from Instagram. Check-ins at various locations or events. You'll see replies to followers. You'll see our (different!) opinions on politics, gaming, and social media. You'll even see the odd quote or thought thrown in for fun and to spark some comments.

What you won't see are tweets that tell people they should be buying our products. (See Figure 10.2.)

Figure 10.2   This isn't the official Nicki Minaj Twitter account but really, who buys from such a spam tweet?

That's not what you should use Twitter for. Use it to build a brand and a community. In time, that will bring you more loyal customers and more sales overall. Joel and Dave have both seen this happen with the ever-increasing number of visitors to their blogs and types of interaction.

But don't panic! This doesn't mean you can't use Twitter to drive direct sales at all. You can, but you have to follow a number of simple rules to maximize the effectiveness of your pitch:

♦ **Don't do it too often.**

A special offer once a week is plenty. More than that and your Twitter timeline will start to look commercial rather than personal. That will reduce your number of users and their level of engagement.

♦ **Make the offers really special.**

Time-limited offers and discount coupons make follow-ers feel that they're being rewarded for reading your tweets. Being part of an exclusive club is a powerful motivator to keep reading.

♦ **Keep the offers targeted.**

People will follow you for all sorts of reasons. They might have seen your Twitter URL on your blog. They might have seen a reply to you in someone else's timeline. Or they could have read one of your retweeted messages.

And they'll stick around because they find your tweets interesting and entertaining.

With a group of followers that could be quite varied, the temptation might be to make offers for any products you can think of. If someone offers you an interesting-looking sales commission (a.k.a. *joint venture*), you might want to mention it on Twitter, offering a discount code, and see whether anyone bites.

You could do that. And some people might click through and buy the product.

But if you keep your offers closely targeted to your primary topic—whatever that subject might be—you'll con-tinue to come across as an expert, and because your trust levels on that topic will be higher, your conversion rates should be higher, too.

♦ **Don't link to a sales page without a special offer.**
Although Twitter users understand that companies are using the service for branding and marketing, they don't want to feel that they're being harassed or pushed into buying. If the tweets are interesting and entertaining, then followers will be happy to read them.

In fact, they'll enjoy following the company on Twitter, and they'll see the company as having its finger on the pulse of its community, a firm that's part of their world and that knows how to follow the community's rules.

Companies that are seen to view followers as nothing more than untapped credit card numbers aren't going to pick up followers. They're actually more likely to lose followers who were loyal customers.

Link directly to a sales page without making the followers feel that they're receiving special treatment, and you create the impression that your focus is on the sale, not the customer.

The best way to drive followers to buying pages is to use the strategies we've seen already: create entertaining tweets, and throw in occasional special offers that appear to reward followers while avoiding the appearance of a hard sell—or even the appearance that you're marketing.

There is one exception, though. A number of timelines have turned up on Twitter that take exactly the opposite approach: they focus almost exclusively on promotions and products but make things fun and lively and give real savings to loyal followers, as shown in Figure 10.3.

Timelines like these have the potential to be good revenue generators. Building up followers will be a challenge, though, because a company with a timeline like this can find *engaging* with followers difficult, which makes building a large follower list difficult, too. You could set up a separate timeline with a mixture of different kinds of tweets as an adjunct to the advert-heavy account, occasionally retweeting and cross-tweeting, but that can be a lot of work.

Figure 10.3   Toys"R"Us (@ToysRUs) sells toys, and it has a lot of fun with its followers, including this treasure hunt, complete with mysterious, unfocused photo.

And, of course, each time you send out an e-mail burst of coupons, you could make sure that it includes your Twitter URL to turn your list subscribers into Twitter followers, too.

Above all, though, you're going to need a regular supply of great offers!

Can You Put Affiliate Links on Twitter?

It's just so tempting. You've spotted a great product, you've got an affiliate code that could land you piles of cash if you can persuade people to buy, and you've got a huge follower list made up of people who could really benefit from the product.

Figure 10.4 Joel sends people to one of his products on Amazon .com by using an affiliate link. #smart.

So all you have to do is toss a short version of the link into one of your tweets, and—presto—piles of cash. Right?

Actually, yes.

Well, okay, there's a little more to it than that.

Just like any item you're hoping to sell through Twitter, affiliate products have to be well targeted to suit your followers. The people who read your tweets should be able to see that you're genuinely interested in helping them rather than making a few bucks. (See Figure 10.4.)

Like affiliate links anywhere, you'll always do better when you recommend the products you're linking to rather than just throw the links at your readers without explanation.

And like any marketing push on Twitter, try not to do it too often, and make sure that you include plenty of other kinds of tweets to soften the marketing effect and increase the feeling that you're recommending a chance find.

If you're in any doubt—or if you find that you start to lose followers after including affiliate links in your timeline—you can always place the link on a Web page and promote that page instead.

Driving Followers to Register

So, you can use Twitter to build a brand, and you can use Twitter to drive followers to buy right away, too.

But there are even more things that you can do with Twitter, and, with the right tweets, you can persuade your followers to take specific actions.

One thing that's become very popular with bloggers, for example, is persuading readers to sign up for their mailing lists or really simple syndication (RSS) feeds. By itself, neither generates revenue. But they both mean that readers are more likely to return, less likely to miss posts, and more likely to click ads or make a purchase down the road.

Persuading followers to do this is very simple. If your followers enjoy your tweets, and if they're clicking through the links to your blog posts, then they're likely to be keen to read more. Sending a tweet pointing out that they can sign up for your list or feed should be enough to persuade many of them to click through and hand over their e-mail addresses.

That's particularly true when you make those invitation tweets look like opportunities for the follower rather than a benefit for you.

When London's Hampstead Theatre (@Hamps_Theatre) wants to have a closer connection with its fans, the organization encourages followers to sign up for the Theatre's mailing list. (See Figure 10.5.)

Figure 10.5 Hampstead Theatre in London makes a not very subtle pitch for subscribers.

Any Twitterer could follow that example or creatively promote his or her mailing list by tweeting something like:

> *That's all for now, I'm off to watch telly. You can read more at [your URL] and don't forget to join the mailing list!*

Do you see how a tweet like that doesn't just recommend that your followers sign up but also leaves them somewhere to go to continue reading your content?

If you can frame your recommendations in a way that looks like you're helping your followers, rather than trying to get them to help you, you'll always get better results.

Tracking Results and Testing Strategies

The success that Joel has enjoyed at Internet marketing didn't come about through good luck.

He might be tempted to say that it happened because he's incredibly talented and interesting, but Dave won't let him get away with it in this book!

In fact, his Web pages started bringing in revenue because Joel's incredibly boring.

Sure, the content he was putting up on his sites was good. It had to be good. Otherwise no one would read it, no matter how well he marketed the site. Reading his site was interesting—at least users thought so. The boring stuff came after the content went up.

Joel would keep a diary that described exactly what each ad unit looked like, where it was located on the page, and what kind of ads it was offering. Next to that description, he would write down exactly how many views those ads received, how many click-throughs ads received, and how much money the page generated.

Then he would change the color or the placement of a few keywords and track the results of the change for a week.

It was painstaking work but a lot more interesting than it sounds. Within a few months he understood what kind of ad formats generated the most click-throughs, in which locations, and with what sort of content. He also knew which subjects gave him the highest-earning keywords.

It was a huge breakthrough, and it meant that he could intelligently target his content and ad space to bring in the maximum revenues. Every time Joel made a change or put up a new Web page, he knew what the result would be.

It didn't give him complete control over all the moneymaking aspects of his website because traffic and Google search rank, like the weather, can be unpredictable. But he got as close as it's possible to get to having complete control, and certainly got to enjoy the rewards.

Joel was able to collect that data because AdSense supplies detailed stats. What Google wasn't showing he could pick up from his Web server logs. With some quick calculations, it became pretty easy to test, track, and record.

Dave's done similar site and traffic analysis, and it's no surprise that both of us are huge fans of testing for any sort of Internet marketing. It's the only way to keep control of your site and avoid wasting time and money on experiments that don't pay off. If you're not earning all the income you think you should be, you can then identify the problem and correct it. The process takes a little while, but once you understand exactly what makes your site tick—and the money flow through—you should have no problem at all keeping it profitable.

The same principle is true on Twitter, but there *is* a problem: Twitter doesn't provide detailed stats.

The only figures that Twitter will tell you are how many people you're following, how many people are following you, and how many updates you've posted. Per tweet, you can see how many times it was retweeted or marked as a favorite or someone responded to it.

In addition, URL shorteners will tell you how many views a link received and how many clicks—that's going to be vital.

That's useful as far as it goes, but it really doesn't go very far.

Testing and tracking on Twitter will involve looking at your Twitter stats, your timeline, and your alerts. It will also involve looking at your server logs.

Twitter alone will be able to tell you:

♦ which kinds of tweets generate the most replies,

♦ which kinds of tweets get the most retweets, and

♦ which replies from which other Twitterers bring you the most followers.

To gather this data, you would need to test different versions of each kind of tweet. Let's say, for example, that you had tweeted something that had little to do with your business but which you thought your followers might find interesting, such as an inspiring quote. (See Figure 10.6.)

You post the tweet, record it in your Twitter journal, and wait a day to see how many replies and retweets that tweet receives.

Now, a day on Twitter can be a long time. On a blog, it usually takes a week to see how a different ad placement or a post on a particular topic affects your revenue, but on Twitter you have to move much faster than that. A day is plenty of time to deliver the data you need.

It *is* possible to post other tweets in the meantime, but when you're testing, we don't recommend it. Followers are more likely to comment on the newer posts than the older ones so you'd skew the results. You might want to set aside one day each week for testing, but change the day regularly so that your followers feel that they should be looking out for your tweets every day.

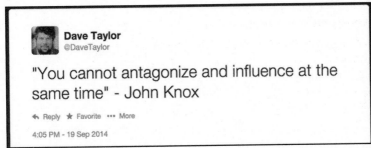

Figure 10.6   What kind of response will this quote have?

Let's say, then, that out of 200 followers, your inspirational quote generates 12 replies, and you can see by searching for your username that it also picked up four retweets. The following week, you might want to try it again with a different quote to see if you get a different result. But let's say you see similar figures.

You also find that although your follower list has been growing at an average of, say, 10 followers per week, the weeks in which you include an inspirational quote give you 13 followers.

So now you can say that tweeting inspirational quotes gives you around 12 replies, four retweets, and three additional followers.

That's valuable information. Now you can compare it with the results of a different kind of tweet. This time you post a tweet that alerts your followers to a new product you're launching. (See Figure 10.7.)

Again, you'll want to:

♦ record the tweet in your journal,

♦ count the number of replies you receive,

♦ note who replied so that you know which of your followers are most likely to respond to your tweets,

Dave Taylor
@DaveTaylor

Heads up, my new Social Media Marketing online course is going to launch in a week. Proven content - hype = Good stuff. #StickAround

↩ Reply ★ Favorite ••• More

4:14 PM - 19 Sep 2014

Figure 10.7   And what does this tweet do . . . ?

♦ track how often the post is mentioned and retweeted based on your username alerts, and

♦ add up the number of new followers you receive in the hours following the post.

That will tell you the effect the tweet has had on your Twitter account. But when you're including a link, you'll also want to know how many people are clicking through. You can discover this from your server logs and from your URL-shortening service, depending on the service you're using.

You might find then that a tweet with a link to a product gives you six replies, including four from regulars; three retweets; and three new followers.

You might also find that according to your server log you got eight click-throughs from Twitter and made two sales.

Now you know that a tweet like that is worth three new followers, a 4 percent click-through rate, *and $60* if the product costs $30.

So, all you have to do is keep sending out tweets like this, and you'll make $60 each time, right?

It's not that easy.

Tracking Multiple Tweets

If you remember just one piece of information from this book, make it this: *tweeting is a process.*

Write a blog post and you can see the results right away. You'll be able to count the views, check the click-throughs, and calculate the value of a post on that topic.

Most important, those figures are relatively consistent.

Although there's no such thing as complete predictability on the Internet, each time you put up a blog post that covers the topic and is optimized in the same way, you should see roughly similar results.

The same isn't true on Twitter.

Discover that a certain kind of tweet gets your followers clicking through to your website and persuades a few of them to buy or click ads, and you might be tempted to do it again a few hours later.

This time, though, instead of picking up three new followers and earning $60 in sales, you get no new followers, one click-through, and no sales.

What went wrong?

It's not the tweet with the link; you've already seen that tweets like these can work.

It was the tweets that came before the link tweet.

Followers don't want to receive the same content all the time on Twitter. And they're not going to click every link you offer them.

If you want to increase the odds that your followers click a link that you offer them on Twitter, make sure that the previous tweets *don't* contain links.

Followers won't be suffering from click fatigue, and because linking isn't something you do too often, the link will appear more valuable.

So if you wanted to post a tweet that drove your followers to a website where you were selling a new e-book or that included a valuable affiliate link, you'd want to prepare the ground with five or six tweets that offer interesting content or that let people know the product is in preparation.

How will you know which kind of content to include?

By looking back at your timeline.

Looking at your timeline will tell you which tweet sequences you've used in the past in the buildup to the link tweet. By comparing those sequences with differences in the click-throughs and conversions from those link tweets, you should be able to see which sequence of tweets is likely to be the most effective.

Let's see how this might work in practice.

Imagine that you're the publisher of a blog about gardening. You use Twitter to build a community of readers, answer questions about gardening issues, mine your followers for knowledge about sourcing seeds and cuttings, and, of course, send them to your blog posts.

You then make an agreement with the author of an e-book on managing a small garden, but before you put up a tweet containing a link to the sales page and urging people to check out a great book, you want to make sure that you get as many click-throughs as possible.

So you look back over your Twitter journal to see which of the tweets you've posted in the past that contained links generated the largest number of click-throughs.

You find that tweet in your timeline, and as well as checking what you wrote in that tweet, you examine what you wrote in the five or six tweets that came before it.

Let's say that those tweets were:

1. "First daffodil of the spring bloomed yesterday. What a sight!"

2. "Thinking of replanting my bonsai. Anyone know which store has the best selection of pots?"

3. "Putting down a new layer of mulch. Whiffy stuff."

4. "Spraying the bougainvillea. I wish it weren't so big and thorny."

5. "A beautiful spring day—warm, sunny, and with just a few clouds. Let's keep the rain off for a few days."

You could then categorize those tweets as:

1. Random thought

2. Question

3. Action

4. Action

5. Random thought

And to increase the chances that your link to the e-book affiliate link would generate at least an equal number of click-throughs, you could repeat the sequence before you posted that tweet:

1. "I love walking around my garden in the evening. It's so quiet and colorful!"

2. "Apple tree is starting to blossom. Anyone know whether the bee population recovered this year?"

3. "Looking at designs for small gardens. So many wonderful new possibilities."

4. "Thinking about laying a new garden path."

5. "Small gardens can look so beautiful . . . when they're well planned."

6. "John Smith has written a wonderful book about miniature gardening. Check it out at http://tinyurl.com/hihiyi."

Is it possible that a different sequence of tweets would have produced more click-throughs? Of course, but when you're Twittering for money, it's a good idea to play it safe—and besides, unless you're tracking the results of your tweets, you won't know which sequence to use!

One of the most enjoyable aspects of using Twitter is that you can do it spontaneously. Maintaining a blog requires thought and planning. The posts themselves take time to research and write, but Twitter is something you can use whenever you feel like it.

That ease of use is part of what makes Twitter so much fun.

Even when you're testing and tracking in the way we've described in this chapter, you can still tweet spontaneously. There's nothing wrong with continuing to post individual tweets as well as tweet sequences.

Nor do you have to record the results of all your tweets. A representative sample should be enough let you understand what different tweets and sequences do.

Tracking can take time and it demands a little attention. But it can identify some fascinating trends, and it means that you can maximize the chances that a tweet will have exactly the effect you want.

As you're recording your tweets, you have to bear another factor in mind, too: *when* you post your tweets.

Unlike blogging, tweeting happens in real time, and it's most effective when your followers are online. There are all sorts of theories about when exactly is the best time to post a tweet. In general, midday and midweek tend to produce the best results, but there is a foolproof method to identify the best time for *your* community: when you find that you're seeing the greatest number of new tweets appearing on your Twitter page, that's always the best time to post tweets that you want your followers to act on.

That's not always easy to assess, especially when you're following lots of people. So focus on a few. Look at when your most important evangelists are online and tweet then. (And the same is true when you're looking to catch the eye of someone else on Twitter: the best time is always when he or she is online and tweeting.)

Making the Most of Twitter's Trends

So far we've been talking about the statistics you can pick up about your own tweets. But there's another kind of data that you can pick up on Twitter.

You can see what topics *other* people are discussing.

Twitter provides some information about trends. You can find a list of trending topics on your Twitter page, and you can see them on the search page. Much more detailed—and far more interesting—is the information provided by third-party data analysis site Trendsmap (www.trendsmap.com). (See Figure 10.8.)

It's all fascinating stuff and you can have a lot of fun tossing in keywords to find out whether "Mac" is more popular than "PC," "trees" is more popular than "flowers," and so on.

But the information you find on Trendsmap can be valuable, too. *It lets you attract lots of followers by tweeting about popular topics, and it means you can tap a known market.*

There are limitations here, of course. Stray too far from the usual subject of your tweets, and you'll struggle to turn readers into followers and struggle even harder to keep them.

And if you simply add a popular hashtag to the end of a tweet that has nothing to do with the topic—as spammers do—you'll do nothing but irritate users. That's no way to succeed on Twitter.

But if you can combine your usual topic with a popular subject—and offer good, unique content—you'll have a passport to the largest discussions currently taking place on Twitter.

Figure 10.8   Trendsmap.com tells you exactly what's hot on Twitter and where!

Let's say, for example, that you're a gardening Twitterer, and you wanted to build up your follower list quickly so that you could get as many people as possible clicking your link.

A glance at your Twitter page shows that the most popular topic currently being discussed on the site is *Gmail* and the second most popular is *themes*. You can't find any reasonable way to link gardening with Gmail, but you could enter a discussion about themes by asking what kind of flower themes people might like to see. (See Figure 10.9.)

A search for the term on Twitter's search engine shows that the themes that people are discussing are, not surprisingly, Gmail's themes. It also shows who's discussing them.

What it won't show, unfortunately, is how many followers those people have. You'll be able to tell that only by clicking through to their tweets until you find someone with a good number of readers and, ideally, a few tweets about gardening, too.

You follow them, then reply to their tweet about themes with a tweet of your own:

> *These themes are cool. Do you know if it's possible to edit them? I'd love to use a pic of my garden.*

Figure 10.9   So, who's talking about themes?

When that Twitterer replies, it should bring a few of his or her followers clicking through to your Twitter page. And because it's a hot topic, *if your tweet is a genuinely valuable contribution,* there's also a good chance that the discussion will spread to other Twitter pages, too, giving you even more followers.

Make this follower-building strategy part of your preparation for an important link tweet, and you'll be able to make the most of a Twitter campaign.

Twitter works in all sorts of wonderful ways. Usually, it works as a fun way for people to keep in touch with others, make new friends, and join discussions. That's how most people use it.

It also works as a tool for mining information and finding expert advice.

And plenty of smart companies are using it to build a brand, turn their customers into a community, and cement the name of their products in the minds of their market.

But it's also possible to use Twitter to prompt people to take a particular course of action.

In this chapter, we've seen how it's possible to use tweets to send people to a blog, to persuade them to buy, and to add them to your e-mail list.

And we've seen how tracking your results and your tweets—and trends, too—can help you get the most out of the actions you want your followers to take.

In the next chapter, we're going to introduce a few strategies that have been known to deliver *instant* results.

11

How to Make Money on Twitter

When Twitter took off, a lot of people saw its business potential right away. They recognized that when a site has millions of members—both individuals and companies—talking and making connections, big deals wouldn't be far off.

But a lot of people got the wrong idea, too. They saw Twitter as a kind of get-rich-quick venue, a place where they could come and immediately make giant piles of cash.

Twitter just doesn't work that way. It's worth reminding you that the power of Twitter lies in the connections you forge and the relationships you build on the site.

Those take time to create. A large following doesn't happen overnight. Tweet well and tweet regularly, and it will happen. But don't expect to have 10,000 followers a week after opening your Twitter account.

And don't expect to close your first deal the day after posting your first tweet.

What Twitter supplies isn't a tool for making money online immediately and with little effort. Truth is, you're not going to be able to create a bunch of Twitter accounts that will allow you to soak up the sun in Waikiki while the revenue continues to flow in all by itself.

Twitter delivers something much more valuable. It provides the basis on which all successful businesses are built.

It delivers trust.

There really aren't many other services that can take entrepreneurs so easily through the process of "Know me. Like me. Trust me. Pay me" and with so many people.

A business built on that foundation and strengthened by a web of good feeling and friendship will always be much more stable than one that relies on quick deal after quick deal.

Stay with us, though. This doesn't mean that earning quick money on Twitter is impossible. It *is* possible. We've already seen that it's possible to drive followers through an affiliate link on the site, but Twitter users have come up with a number of other methods to turn their Twitter presence into instant cash.

In this chapter, we're going to explain how the most effective of those strategies work. You can use some or all of them if you want to. They're already making decent amounts of money for some people, and there's no reason they can't make a little extra cash for you, too.

But if you are going to use these methods, make sure they form just part of your Twitter strategy rather than define your entire Twitter presence. If all you do is use Twitter to try to make a quick buck, it won't work, and you'll be missing a giant marketing opportunity.

Earn with Advertising on Twitter

Advertising has always seemed like the most obvious way to make money out of a Twitter timeline. If you can generate income by placing ads in front of blog readers—and you can certainly do that!—then surely you can also make money by placing ads in front of your Twitter followers.

Or maybe not. A blog page has all sorts of elements. You can place ads in different places and in a number of different ways, from the subtle to the overt. But the idea is always to make them unobtrusive. The better you integrate your ads into your Web page design, the more people will click on them and the more money you'll make.

On Twitter, though, there's no way to make the ads unobtrusive. Worse, there's always the fear that an ad will put readers off. It's as though you were holding a conversation with someone, and then you broke off suddenly to recommend that he or she buy a can of Coca-Cola or use a particular credit card.

It's not the kind of thing that makes for a smooth conversation. On Twitter's side, it's the concern that if users won't accept ads in timelines, they'll stop using the service. Individual users might just stop following you, but that's painful, too!

In practice, those fears have turned out to be largely unfounded. A number of services have turned up that deliver ads from advertisers to Twitterers, and provided it's done carefully, their services can provide positive results. All the major services work with the entire range of your social media presence (that is, Facebook, Google Plus, Instagram, Pinterest, etc.). But Twitter is definitely part of that, and there are promos that are sent out offering money per tweet.

One company that covers this area well is IZEA (formerly SponsoredTweets.com), but the fact is, with the widespread use of the #spon, #sponsored, or #ad hashtag, it's easy to search Twitter and see who's getting paid to share an advertiser's message with followers. (See Figure 11.1.)

Figure 11.1 Sponsored tweets can come from many sources, and they're now a common part of the Twitter world. This is the result of a search for "#spon."

First, effective advertising on Twitter requires 100 percent disclosure. For this kind of advertising, that's vital. That's the #spon, #sponsored, or #ad hashtag.

When either of us shares an affiliate link on a website, it always points to a product that we have used, have tested, and feel comfortable recommending. If we're not certain that our readers would benefit from using that product, we wouldn't advertise it.

But sometimes Joel and Dave haven't used the products advertised in their timelines. In that situation, it's important that people don't think that we're recommending them. In other words, it's important that followers can quickly identify sponsored or affiliate posts and differentiate them from the usual posts and tweets. (See Figure 11.2.)

Not every advert posted is clearly marked as an ad, but it's exactly what the Federal Trade Commission (FTC) requires. Any reputable sponsorship site or service, such as IZEA, makes the process automatic.

You might think that adding *#spon* or *#ad* might make the ad less effective, but it does make it more honest. As Joel says, he'd rather lose a few bucks than lose the trust of his followers. That's worth a lot more.

Some Twitter and general social media advertising systems require you to hand over your password so that they can insert ads automatically and with hardly any restrictions into your timeline.

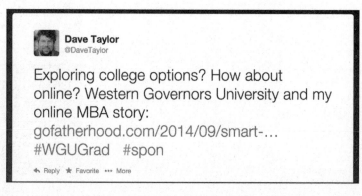

Figure 11.2   A sponsored tweet as it appeared in Dave's timeline. Note his use of *#spon* to help people identify it as such.

That's a bad idea. Never share your password. But even if they use what's called OAuth to gain approval from you to inject tweets on your behalf, we still don't recommend it: you don't want a company placing sales messages in your Twitter timeline unless you've had a chance to review them first.

When you sign up for IZEA (http://comm.us/izea), you'll be asked to choose between posting ads that you write, ads that the advertiser writes, or both of those options. Initially at least, you should be choosing to write the ads yourself. They'll still be marked as ads but you'll be in control. If you manage to build a relationship with an advertiser, then at some point you might trust the company enough to let it write the ads. But at the beginning, write them yourself. They'll have your voice, so they'll be less obtrusive. Your click-throughs will be higher, too.

You also get to set the price. That's vital, too.

IZEA, and similar services, pay in two ways. They pay on a cost-per-thousand (known as CPM) basis for each tweet that you show, or they pay on a cost-per-click (known as CPC) basis that delivers a flat fee for every follower who goes to the advertiser's website from your link.

You get to set those rates. That means you're never earning less than you think your timeline is worth.

Calculating those figures, though, isn't easy. Internet marketer and blogger John Chow (@JohnChow) has been known to charge $250 per tweet on a timeline with almost 100,000 followers. That might not sound like much per follower, but it can still deliver a sizeable sum simply for writing a tweet. The amount will vary depending on the subject you tweet about, the number of followers, and the value of your brand. If you're tweeting legal or financial advice, and you're well-known and trusted with a strong brand name, you should find that advertisers are prepared to pay a great deal.

The same is true of the amount you want to charge on a per-click basis. The best way to figure out this amount is to open a Google AdWords account first. Use the keyword tool to generate keyword tags for your IZEA account, and use the estimated average cost per click for each of those keywords to produce a quote that lies in the middle of the range. Google will be one of your competitors, so those are the prices you're competing against.

You'll need at least 200 followers to qualify for any sort of Twitter ad campaign, and the account needs to be at least four months old. Once you start receiving the ads, pay attention to your follower numbers. If you find that the number falls significantly after an ad appears, then ask your followers what happened.

That's what's great about Twitter. On a website, it's very difficult to get feedback from your readers about their reactions to an ad. You're largely restricted to looking at stats and trying to figure out what's happening. On Twitter, you can ask your readers what they think and see whether they found the ad helpful or obtrusive. You might find that it's the advertiser or the copy, not the ad itself, that was causing the problem.

Barter, Buy, and Sell Your Way to Profit

Twitter is full of opportunities, and just as people have managed to make livings out of buying and selling on eBay, so also it's possible to make money out of the arbitrage opportunities that have now cropped up on Twitter.

This is all very straightforward. You're going to be looking for products that you can buy for a price lower than you know you can sell it for elsewhere.

The best places to browse are the many Twitter timelines that act as classifieds. You can find a list of these by doing a Google— or Twitter—search, but you can also check out Twellow, the Twitter directory.

Daype, for example, is a classifieds service that competes with Craigslist but also has an active Twitter stream. Bear in mind, too, that a number of other classified sites and even newspaper services stream additions to their listings directly to Twitter, giving you a huge choice of items to browse from your home page.

In effect, by looking for and then following a range of different classified timelines, you'll have created one central place to view items listed for sale.

As always, the key to success with this kind of arbitrage is to know the prices in one small niche. Try to spot a bargain in a field about which you know little, and it's likely that you'll be paying the market rate. Specialize in one type of product, whether that's DC comics, Mustang cars, or Barbie dolls, and you should find it easier to spot the underpriced goods and generate a profit when you sell it elsewhere.

With such a huge number of products flowing through Twitter, you might even want to create a set of people you're following specifically for trading. That will prevent your main home page from being swamped with for sale offers, drowning out your other

Figure 11.3   Want to buy a cute ballerina bear?

messages. But because it won't always be possible to filter the types of classifieds you're seeing, you might struggle to find the items you really want.

Some popular hashtags also help keep things organized in the Twitterverse. Search for "#forsale" and you might be surprised at what shows up (see Figure 11.3).

For eBay traders in particular, Twitter can massively broaden the sources of the goods they buy and visibility of those that they sell.

And if you don't want to pay for those goods, there's always the option of bartering. As well as straightforward classifieds on Twitter, you can also find plenty of people offering services and goods in return for things they need. You're not going to get rich this way, but you might find that you're able to trade something of little value to you for something that you value far more. That's a profitable trade.

Twitter is not a get-rich-quick scheme at all, and thinking about it that way is only going to lead to disappointment. It's a place to get to know people and build the relationships that lead to long-term deals. These simple examples may help you make a little extra money on Twitter, but they're not what makes Twitter useful for entrepreneurs.

In the next chapter, we'll look at some of the tools that make Twitter even more useful.

12

Beyond Twitter.com: Third-Party Tools You Will Want to Know About

One of the things that really makes Twitter fun is that it comes with lots of optional add-ons. Twitter allows programmers to write applications that anyone can use and that extend the power of the service.

Some of them are a little odd. We've yet to find a good use for Twitter in Second Life. But some of them are extremely helpful. All sorts of applications let you send and follow tweets without opening your browser, for example.

That makes for hours of exciting experimentation—just the sort of thing that tech-minded people love to do.

On the other hand, if you want to skip straight to the most useful apps, here are some that we recommend.

SocialOomph

Follow someone on Twitter and there's a good chance that he or she will follow you in return. It's not guaranteed, but it does happen a lot. It's why one strategy to pick up followers is to do a lot of following.

The reason it happens a lot is that reciprocal following looks like good manners. If someone's following you, then it seems only

Figure 12.1   SocialOomph also lets you schedule your tweets in advance.

right you should follow him or her back. As we've seen, that might not be the smartest move—it can make you look like a spammer, and you can't possibly follow everyone on a long list closely—but many people do it anyway.

And one reason they do it is that it's easy. SocialOomph (www .SocialOomph.com) lets you set up autofollows. Whenever someone follows you, you'll automatically follow him or her in return.

That can be a neat trick, but it's not the service's main function.

The biggest reason for using SocialOomph is that it lets you set up tweets in advance—a bit like an autoresponder. (See Figure 12.1.)

Now that really can be valuable.

It means that you can keep your timeline ticking over even while you're sleeping, working your day job, or spending the weekend with the kids. You wouldn't want to create a false impression on your timeline by preparing tweets that say you're hard at work on a blog post while in fact you're relaxing at a spa, but you can prepare some random thoughts and other tweets to keep your timeline active.

Best of all, you can use SocialOomph to prepare a series of tweets that lead up to a link you want your followers to click through.

SocialOomph also provides keyword alerts, which can be useful, and automatic thank-yous to followers, which you need to use carefully. Fill your timeline with personal thank-yous, and your tweets look dull for everyone else. SocialOomph recommends sending your welcome messages by direct message, but we don't think that's a good idea either. You can save the reward of a mention for people who reply to your tweets or say something nice about your product. The biggest reward comes when you make your gratitude public.

SocialOomph is free and available at www.SocialOomph.com, but you might also want to check out Twittertise (www.twittertise .com). This does almost exactly the same thing but also lets you see the number of click-throughs on links that you insert into the tweet.

Twitterrific

Twitter might have been designed with mobiles in mind, but it was never very mobile friendly. Dialing a number every time you wanted to send a tweet was a bit of a nuisance, and what if you wanted to send a direct message or reply to a friend's tweet, let alone see all his or her tweets?

Fortunately, developers have come up with some neat alternatives.

Twitterrific is a Twitter client that sits on a Mac's desktop. It shows tweets from your followers and lets you tweet back in return. The interface is attractive and fun, and the program means you don't have to work with your Twitter page open in your browser. (See Figure 12.2.)

Best of all, Twitterrific is also available for the iPhone. It even comes with a minibrowser so that you don't lose your timeline every time you click a link, and it lets followers see where you are.

Figure 12.2   Twitterrific puts Twitter in your pocket.

It's a very neat solution for Twitterers on the move. Twitterrific is available for download from Icon Factory at http://iconfactory .com/software/twitterrific. The free version is funded by ads, but you can get an ad-free version for just a few bucks.

Twhirl

Twitterrific might be very cool and a neat solution for iPhone users (Tweetie, available from the iPhone app store, is great, too.) Owners of other kinds of mobile phones can try TwitterMail (www .twittermail.com) for e-mail-enabled phones, Cellity (www.cellity .com) for Java-enabled phones, and Blackbird (http://dossy.org/ twitter/blackbird/) for BlackBerry phones.

For desktop Twitterers, Twitterrific is also limited; it works only on the Mac. PC users have to look elsewhere for a Twitter client. Many of them look to Seesmic's Twhirl.

Like Twitterrific, Twhirl frees Twitterers from Twitter's Web page, letting them send and receive tweets from an attractive instant message–style client. It's packed with all sorts of other useful goodies too, such as automatic short uniform resource locators (URLs), search, and image posting to TwitPic. It's built on Adobe AIR, so you'll have to download that first, but both are free and available from http://twhirl.en.softonic.com/.

Twitterfeed

We mentioned Twitterfeed in Chapter 9. Spend any time at all reading tweets, and you're going to come across plenty of examples of its use.

As a way of adding one particular type of content to your timeline, Twitterfeed can be very useful. But do bear in mind that the price you're paying for the ease of providing blog updates through Twitter is a loss of the personal touch. If your blog is hugely popular, you can get away with a Twitterfeed timeline dedicated solely to informing followers of your latest posts.

For most people, though, Twitterfeed's updates become just one kind of tweet but one that they can set up and leave.

Sign up for free at www.twitterfeed.com. (See Figure 12.3.)

Trendistic

A number of different services allow Twitterers to keep track of the popularity of various topics and keywords on Twitter. Some use a frequently updated tag cloud to show relative popularity, but we like the graphs on Trendistic. They're accurate and detailed, and you can make comparisons between different terms and even see samples of the tweets you're examining. (See Figure 12.4 on page 245.)

Trendistic can be a very useful way to make sure that you're targeting the most popular terms and look for other people Twittering about your topic.

It looks very neat, too.

Use it at trendistic.com.

Figure 12.3   Twitterfeed allows you to add a feed to your Twitter timeline.

Twellow

Trendistic can help you find people with similar interests to your own, but Twellow makes it all much, much easier. Run by Web-ProNews, it's supposed to be a kind of *Yellow Pages* of social media, but it operates more like a Twitter Yahoo! (See Figure 12.5 on page 246.)

The site tracks conversations on Twitter and places the Twitterers behind them into various categories. Click one of those categories and you'll be able to see a list of suitable Twitterers, complete with sample tweet, bio, image, and the number of their followers.

For Twitterers looking for interesting and useful people to follow, it's a fantastic resource.

And clearly, for Twitterers who want to be followed, it's hugely valuable, too.

Figure 12.4   Trendistic makes looking at graphs fun.

Once you start sending tweets, you should find that you're added automatically, but if you can't find your name on the site, you can add it yourself. In any case, it's certainly worth checking the categories that you've been listed under and self-editing them if necessary.

Keep Twellow close by at www.twellow.com.

TweetBeep

Twellow tells you who tends to talk about what, but you'll also want to know who's talking about your topics now.

TweetBeep, which sends out regular alerts whenever a keyword is used on Twitter, is really a must for anyone thinking about marketing through microblogging.

Remember that tracking your username or your company name and diving right into a conversation can look a little creepy.

Figure 12.5   Twellow: Twitter's *Yellow Pages.*

If you see someone has mentioned you, it's often a good idea to follow him or her before replying.

You can set up your alerts at www.tweetbeep.com.

TwitterCounter

There's one more useful matrix you might want to know when you're looking for people to follow, though—and when you want to know how you're doing—and that's the rate of follower growth.

When you're tracking your own tweets and their results, you should have those figures handy, but when you look at others' profiles, there's no way of knowing whether they picked up all of their followers a year ago or whether their tweets are still generating interest.

TwitterCounter lets you see anyone's follower numbers over time. (See Figure 12.6.)

Figure 12.6   Numbers aren't everything on Twitter, but
TwitterCounter's growth charts can provide some interesting stats.

Just toss a name into the site, and you'll receive a graph showing how his or her follower numbers have risen and fallen over the past week.

It's interesting and, when you're looking for people on the up to follow and be followed by, useful, too.

Have fun at www.twittercounter.com.

TweetDeck

Twitter's strength is its simplicity. Short posts, short replies, and quick conversations make for a service that's simple to use. But it's also very limited. It's not easy to keep track of conversations, for example. You'll be holding multiple chats with multiple followers all at the same time and often on different topics. As one tweet comes in, the last one will pushed down the list, making it difficult to follow the course of an exchange.

Nor does Twitter allow you to group tweets according to subject.

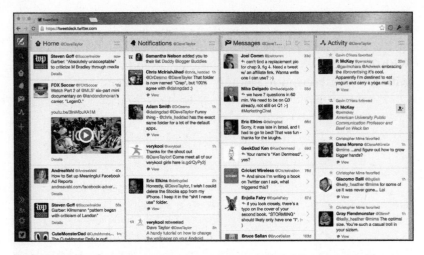

Figure 12.7   TweetDeck supplies a control panel for multitasking Twitterers.

TweetDeck lets you do that. (See Figure 12.7.)

This service really is a must-have for anyone with a large list of followers. You can create multiple columns and group them according to topics. It's the closest you're likely to get to Facebook's groups.

It's also very useful for following hashtag chats and current events. Because the tweets are updated in real time, you'll be able to keep up with conversations and updates without refreshing the page.

You'll need to download Adobe AIR again, but it's still free and available at www.tweetdeck.com.

As of this writing, Joel has begun beta testing another desktop-based Twitter client that may one-up TweetDeck. It's called TweetGlide (http://tweetglide.com/index.php), and it may well be worth a look.

TwitThis

TwitThis isn't exactly a Twitter application, but it's certainly useful nonetheless and should be a basic tool for any Twitter-based marketer.

You've probably seen all the buttons at the bottom of blog posts, urging people to Digg the article or send it to StumbleUpon. With TwitThis, you can also ask them to send a URL of the page with a brief description to their Twitter followers.

It's a simple and effective way to help your blog or website make the most of Twitter's viral power.

Load up on your buttons at www.twitthis.com.

TweetAways

One of the most powerful marketing uses of Twitter has been contests and giveaways. Companies have managed to drum up huge amounts of publicity and exposure by giving away everything from books and show tickets to cameras and computers. The usual method is to ask people to follow you, retweet a message (often with a link), and include a hashtag to make it easy to identify. One tweet is then picked at random at a set time and the winner notified by direct message.

It's very straightforward and the viral power is clear. It takes only a few people to tell their followers that they're hoping to win whatever it is you're giving away for the message to spread right across Twitter. And the more valuable the item you're offering, the faster and further you'll find it spreads.

The tricky bit, though, is choosing a winner, and that's where services such as TweetAways come in so useful. They'll do all the hard work for you. They'll keep track of all of the tweets that qualify, then choose one at random at the time you select. All you have to do is collect the name and address and arrange the shipping.

You can find it at www.tweetaways.com.

Hootsuite

Hootsuite is a comprehensive Twitter client for serious business Twitterers. It allows multiple Twitterers to operate the same account, keep track of more than one timeline, follow statistics, and monitor their brands—and do it all in one place. (See Figure 12.8.)

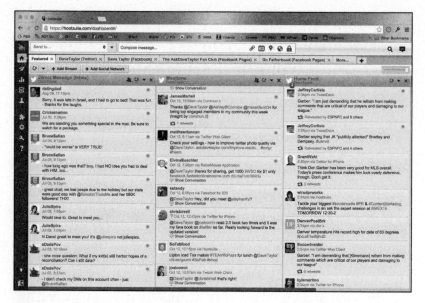

Figure 12.8   HootSuite calls itself the "professional Twitter client."

Once you're using Twitter seriously for marketing, there's a good chance that you'll find yourself using Hootsuite—especially because it's free. It just makes doing all of those essential elements that are a part of using Twitter for business so much easier.

Download it from www.hootsuite.com.

*   *   *

This is just a number of the most useful tools that we've found for Twitter. There are plenty of others, and new ones are coming out every day with better interfaces, more features, and neater designs.

You can have hours of fun just downloading them and trying them out until you create the tool kit that works best for you. Because many of them are similar, much comes down to personal taste.

On the whole, though, your toolkit should contain applications that let you find people to follow, track keywords, organize your followers, and tweet and reply easily. Those are the basics.

Directory of Recommended Twitter Members to Follow

In putting together a directory of people to follow, we realize that such a directory could be several complete volumes. Depending on your market or niche, with more than 250 million active members, you might imagine that quite a few people are using Twitter in a meaningful way.

So it made sense that we share with you those people whom *we* follow. That means you are likely to encounter a lot of other social media or business people here, rather than the big-name celebrities with millions of followers. This list is alphabetical by first name, and by no means is it exhaustive. However, we think the following people are pretty cool and worthy of your follow.

Adam Helweh — @secretsushi

Adryenn Ashley — @adryenn

Amber Ludwig Vilhauer — @AmberVilhauer

Andy Grignon — @pre_me

Ann Handley — @MarketingProfs

Bob Burg — @BobBurg

Brendon Burchard — @BrendonBurchard

Brian Carter — @briancarter

Brian Clark — @copyblogger

Brian Fanzo — @iSocialFanz

Brian Moran — @brianmoran

Brian Solis — @briansolis

Bryan Kramer — @bryankramer

Carrie Wilkerson — @CarrieWilkerson

Charles Garcia — @charlespgarcia

Charles Trippy — @CharlesTrippy

Chris Brogan — @chrisbrogan

Chris Heuer — @chrisheuer

Chris Voss — @CHRISVOSS

Cliff Ravenscraft — @GSPN

Colin Sprake — @ColinSprake

Dave Cox — @davecox

Dave Kerpen — @davekerpen

Dave Peck — @davepeck

David H. Lawrence XVII — @dhlawrencexvii

David Mathison — @BeTheMedia

David Meerman Scott — @dmscott

Deb Cole — @CoachDeb

Dino Dogan — @dinodogan

E. Brian Rose — @EBrianRose

Ekaterina Walter — @Ekaterina

Gary Vaynerchuk — @garyvee

Gina Carr — @GinaCarr

James Hickey — @sdentrepreneur

Jay Baer — @jaybaer

Jen Groover — @jengroover

Jennifer Walsh — @BehindTheBrand

Jessica Northey — @JessicaNorthey

Joe Wood — @pastorjoewood

John Chow — @JohnChow

John Kremer — @JohnKremer

John Lee Dumas — @johnleedumas

John Nosta — @JohnNosta

John Oliver — @iamjohnoliver

John Rampton — @johnrampton

Kare Anderson — @KareAnderson

Keith Ferrazzi — @ferrazzi

Ken McArthur — @KenMcArthur

Ken Surritte — @ksurritte

Kim Garst — @kimgarst

Laura Fitton — @Pistachio

Lewis Howes — @LewisHowes

Lori Moreno — @LoriMoreno

Lori Ruff — @loriruff

Lou Mongello — @loumongello

Marc Ensign — @MarcEnsign

Mari Smith — @MariSmith

Mark Babbitt — @MarkSBabbitt

Mark Schaefer — @markwschaefer

Marsha Collier — @MarshaCollier

Michael Gerber — @michaelEGerber

Michael Hyatt — @MichaelHyatt

Michael A. Stelzner — @Mike_Stelzner

Neal Schaffer — @NealSchaffer

Neil Patrick Harris — @ActuallyNPH

Peg Fitzpatrick — @PegFitzpatrick

Perry Hewitt — @perryhewitt

Peter Shankman — @petershankman

Rachel Haot — @rachelhaot

Rachel Martin — @finding_joy

Ray Edwards — @RayEdwards

Reg Saddler — @zaibatsu

Richard Branson — @richardbranson

Rick Warren — @RickWarren

Robert Scoble — @Scobleizer

Sally Hogshead — @SallyHogshead

Sarah Evans — @prsarahevans

Scott Levy — @FuelOnline

Scott Stratten — @unmarketing

Shawne Duperon — @ShawneTV

Sheila Simkin — @sheilatravels

Steve Farnsworth — @Steveology

Steve Strauss — @SteveStrauss

Sue B. Zimmerman — @SueBZimmerman

Ted Coiné — @tedcoine

Ted Rubin — @TedRubin

Terry Brock — @TerryBrock

Thomas Hawk — @thomashawk

Tim Washer — @timwasher

Todd Wilms — @toddmwilms

Tom Hanks — @tomhanks

Tom Ziglar — @TomZiglar

Tony Hsieh — @tonyhsieh

Viveka von Rosen — @LinkedInExpert

Warren Whitlock — @WarrenWhitlock

Index

Index

3 1901 05772 3068